MW01103980

THE NEW CREATORS

OF

EMPOWERED

WORKERS

The New Creators of Empowered Workers

The Supervisors GUIDE to Managing

By Lloyd Pressel, Ph.D., & Robert H. Gardner

Loma Linda Publishers, Bisbee, Arizona
Box AA
BISBEE, ARIZONA 85603
602-432-5361

THE NEW CREATORS OF
EMPOWERED WORKERS

The Supervisor's GUIDE to Managing

By Lloyd Pressel, Ph. D., & Robert H. Gardner

Published by: Loma Linda Publishers
Box AA
Bisbee, Arizona 85603, U.S.A.

All rights reserved. No part of this book may be reproduced or transmitted in any form or by any means, electronic or mechanical, including photocopying and recording, or by information storage and retrieval system without written permission from the authors, except for the inclusion of brief quotations in a review.

Copyright © 1993 by Lloyd Pressel and Robert H. Gardner

Printed in the United States of America

Library of Congress Cataloguing in Publication Data:

Pressel, Lloyd
Gardner, Robert H.
        The New Creators of Empowered Workers
        The Supervisor's GUIDE to Managing

    1. Supervision
    2. Worker Empowerment
    3. Self-Managed Teams
    4. Leadership

I. Management, Participation
658.315'2dc20   93-077581
ISBN 0-9634821-4-9 Hardcover

DISCLAIMER

This book is designed to provide information in regard to the subject matter covered. Every effort has been made to make this book as accurate as possible. However, there may be mistakes, both typographical and in content. The purpose of the book is to inform, educate and provide a general guide for helping supervisors empower and lead workers. The authors and Loma Linda Publishers shall have neither liability nor responsibility to any person or entity with respect to any loss or damage caused or alleged to be caused directly or indirectly by the information contained in this book.

CONTENTS

CONTENTS (Continued)

1

SO NOW YOU'RE A BOSS

You may be a factory supervisor, boss of a construction crew, head nurse, office services supervisor, maitre d' or first chef, or in any other supervisory position where you have people working under you.

You might have been promoted yesterday or some time ago, but in any case, you're part of management now. If you're like most other first-line supervisors, you worked your way up out of the ranks by doing your job well. Your technical knowledge and ability to handle paper work are important, but the really challenging part of your job now is to get good work out of your people.

You may feel sometimes that you're still not very high on the totem pole of your organization. But take a look at the chart below showing how a typical company employing 5,000 breaks down as to numbers in management and number of rank and file workers.

EMPLOYEE DISTRIBUTION*		
Top Management Chairmen, Presidents, Vice Presidents, Division heads	15	0.3 %
Department heads, other middle managers	50	1 %
Supervisors, Foremen	450	9 %
Rank & file workers	4,485	89.7 %
	5,000	100 %

% based on our experience with 500 firms

These proportions stay about the same in most manufacturing and other line organizations, such as hospitals and governmental agencies.

YOU HAVE POWER

As a first-line supervisor, you're part of the relatively small group that runs the business and wields the power of the organization over the workforce, and that's a lot of power. What's more, you in the first level of supervision have more influence and control over workers than the rest of management, because you have the direct contact.

To those under you, you're it. You're the part of the company they see and live with every day. **You** -- not company policies or employee manuals or what the president says -- **create the work environment where they spend half of their waking hours.**

It can be a positive and healthy work environment where they feel good about themselves and about you, and where they want to do their best. Or it can be a negative environment in which they feel put down, resentful and powerless. **It depends on you.**

If your subordinates like and respect you, they'll give you a full day's work for a day's pay, and even more. If they don't, they'll do just enough work to keep from getting fired, and you've got a problem.

A poll by a national survey group showed that only 4% of American workers like their bosses. Most workers, it appears, aren't getting the kind of leadership they need and want to turn on their full capacity. Why not?

In the next few pages, think about what it takes to bring out the best in you, both in relation to your present job and back in the days when you were a worker on the line. Check whether you tend to agree or disagree with each of the following statements. (Substitute "her" for "his" where appropriate, of course.)

1. I perform best when my boss tells me exactly what to do and how to do it.

_____ Agree   _____ Disagree

2. I perform best when my boss lays out what has to be done and then leaves it up to me how to do it.

_____ Agree   _____ Disagree

3. If I make a mistake, I expect my boss to bawl me out, tell me where I went wrong and what I'm to do in the future.

_____ Agree   _____ Disagree

4. If I make a mistake, I want my boss to call it to my attention and then tell me to figure out how I'm going to avoid making the same mistake again.

_____ Agree   _____ Disagree

5. A boss should keep his distance from his subordinates in order to maintain a position of authority.

_____ Agree   _____ Disagree

6. People work better if a boss is friendly toward them, calls them by name and gets to know them personally.

_____ Agree   _____ Disagree

7. If I do my job well, that's what I'm being paid for, and I don't expect any special praise for it.

_____ Agree   _____ Disagree

8. If I'm doing my job well, I expect my boss to take note of it and compliment me for it.

_____ Agree   _____ Disagree

9. If I'm having some trouble at home that bothers me, I should keep it to myself and not let it get in the way of doing my job..

_____ Agree   _____ Disagree

10. If I'm having some trouble at home, I'd like to be able to talk it over with my boss.

_____ Agree   _____ Disagree

11. Everybody in a company has his own job to do and shouldn't stick his nose into other people's business.

_____ Agree   _____ Disagree

12. If I see some improvement that might be made in tools or procedures, whether or not it relates to my specific job, I should be able to tell my boss about it and know that it will get the right attention.

_____ Agree   _____ Disagree

13. Workers in my group are different from me in the way they they think and feel.

_____ Agree   _____ Disagree

14. My workers are a lot like me.

_____ Agree   _____ Disagree

You might have had trouble deciding whether you agree or disagree 100% with these statements. That's good. The best supervisors don't go by the book but are able to judge how rules apply. In seminars for supervisors, we encourage round table discussion of questions like these. That's where people sort out their old beliefs and open their minds to new ideas. As you go through these pages, we hope you'll do the same.

In this chapter, you've begun to look at yourself to see what turns you on or off. Assuming you were once a worker on the line yourself, you thought about what you liked or didn't like about your old boss and how you feel about the boss you have now. Have you been treated the way you think you should be treated to bring out the best in you, or is there a better way?

In the next chapter, we'll be looking at the people who work for you, what they need and want in their jobs, and what they expect of you as a boss.

4

2

THE MANAGER DIFFERENCE

In the first chapter, if you agreed that the workers in your group are a lot like you, you're right on track with what we know about human nature.

People are alike in many ways, but on the job, you are different from the rest of your group in one important respect. You are the boss. You have an authority over them that they do not have over you. That's the manager difference.

In an organization, everybody has a boss. Not everybody in the organization, however, is a boss. In fact, as we saw in the first chapter, 90% of employed people have no authority over anyone else. First-line supervisors are in that 10% who make up management, and there are six times as many of you as there are in all the rest of management put together.

In a broad sense, the organization itself has a boss --the customers for its products or the publics to whom its renders services. It has to satisfy their wants and needs at prices they can pay. If it doesn't do this, or can't do it and still make a profit to sustain it in the long run, sooner or later it will go out of business.

In order to function, all organizations need control over the people who work for them. That's how the boss idea got started. A key requirement for any boss is to keep control of subordinates so that they work together toward the organization goals.

Think through this need of the organization for control that stands in conflict with the workers' yearning for some control over what's happening to them. People are willing to give up a lot of control in return for a job and a paycheck, but they don't want to give up all of it. To be completely under the domination of someone else is to give up their vitality. All need some control over how they do their work to make them feel their worth..

How can these two needs for control be blended together for the benefit of both? **It's done by those first-line supervisors who know how to draw out the creative ideas of their work groups and direct them into productive channels.** Everybody wins. Workers have a say in what they do, yet the organization winds up with better control than it had before. Learning how to involve workers and make them a part of the whole production process is the challenge and obligation of first-line supervisors today.

Here's a list of things that are usually important to workers. How do you think the **workers** under you would rate them in order of importance? Rank them 1 to 10, then read the next chapter.

_____ Good wages

_____ Full appreciation of work done

_____ Job security

_____ Good working conditions

_____ Effective appeal of alleged injustices

_____ Promotion and growth within the company

_____ Tactful disciplining

_____ Feeling "in" on things

_____ Interesting work

_____ Personal loyalty to other employees

6

3

KNOW YOUR PEOPLE

At the end of the last chapter, you ranked how your people rated their concerns in order of importance. A national research organization has given this test to managers and supervisors like you in several hundred companies through the United States. Then they gave the same test to workers themselves. Compare the two sets of ratings in the tables below, then check them against your own rankings to see how close you came to understanding what workers want and need.

Ranking by Employees		Ranking by Management
1	Full appreciation of work done	7
2	Feeling "in" on things	10
3	Effective appeal of alleged injustice	8
4	Job security	2
5	Good wages	1
6	Interesting work	6
7	Promotion and growth within the company	4
8	Personal loyalty to other employees	9
9	Good working conditions	3
10	Tactful disciplining	5

The surprising thing is that the results have been virtually the same wherever the test has been administered over the past years. **Apparently, management is misreading the minds of its workers.** What is the reason for this?

TIMES HAVE CHANGED

One reason is that times have changed. In the early years of this century, wages were low and working conditions in mines, stockyards and many factories were terrible. Unions fought to improve them and won. Then we went through the Depression, when jobs disappeared and wages fell. We got Social Security, unemployment compensation, OSHA, the minimum wage and other legislation that helped workers. Many of their earlier demands have been answered, so they are no longer at the top of their "wish" list.

In the 1960s, young people began to assert their rights as individuals and to revolt against "the establishment." The hippie movement died down, but it left workers with new expectations of what a job ought to mean. They wanted more from their work than wages. They were looking for recognition, a sense of being part of the action, a right to be heard, and more control over their own lives in how they did their work. All these aspirations are reflected in the way workers rank their priorities.

Management by and large hasn't caught up with these shifts in employee attitudes. One reason may be that many in senior management and supervisory positions today were trained in old ways of bossing, when wages and working conditions were the main concerns of workers and they didn't expect much else. As new supervisors (you, perhaps) came up out of the ranks, they found a mindset in the management organization that favored the status quo and discouraged change. New bosses followed old models, with the result that management and the new generation of workers have grown further and further apart.

Many unions, too, have failed to change with the times. Labor negotiations still focus on old issues, such as wages and work rules. This is understandable. How are you going to bargain for such things as appreciation and respect? Union membership has been steadily shrinking for years, largely because unions find it increasingly difficult to deliver what workers really want. If management would wake up to the fact that **they** can answer the needs of the workplace and would take the right steps to do so, unions and management would find it easier to work together.

Worker priorities may change in the future as they have in the past, of course. The downsizing of companies, layoffs and elimination of jobs through technology could make job security a bigger issue than its fourth place ranking would indicate. When the business cycle comes around as usual, new jobs will be generated to take up the slack in employment, and we would expect the basic needs of workers to remain about as the poll tells us.

YOU MAKE THE DIFFERENCE

In reality, you're the only one who can make a difference, because you and supervisors like you are the only ones who are in direct, daily touch with all the workers.

No one else in the organization is in a position to know your workers the way you do. You are the one they look to. **For them, you are the company.** Donald Peterson, now retired as chairman of Ford, used to go around the plants talking to people and giving them a pat on the back. It was a morale builder, but he couldn't do it everywhere every day. That's your job.

A lot of supervisors hang back from getting to know their workers and establishing a good relationship with them, not because they don't want to, but because they don't know how. **The ideas in this book provide a blueprint on how to be a good people manager.** Following the blueprint will benefit you, your people and your organization.

WHAT ARE YOUR RESPONSIBILITIES?

Rank the following in order of importance. If you think some of them are not part of your job, mark them with an "x." Add any you think are missing on the lines at the bottom.

_____ Planning each day's work so that it gets done on schedule.

_____ Seeing that machines and equipment are kept in good working condition and that the right kind and amount of supplies are on hand.

_____ Passing along instructions and communications from management to workers in my group.

_____ Disciplining workers who get out of line.

_____ Instructing new workers in doing their job.

_____ Interviewing prospective new hires and making recommendations to management.

_____ Firing poor workers or recommending that they be fired.

_____ Looking for new or better ways to do things.

_____ Encouraging suggestions from my workers on new or better ways to do things.

_____ Attending meetings with my boss or management.

_____ Seeing that workers in my group meet quality standards.

_____ Listening to workers' personal problems.

_____ Other

_____

_____

_____

_____

4

YOU AND YOUR JOB

Before you read this chapter, study the questionnaire on the opposite page. This will help define what **you** consider to be your main responsibilities. If you add some items not shown, that's good, because it indicates you're thinking about **your** job and what you actually do.

Supervisors often think of their responsibilities as mainly technical and administrative. The reason for this is that upper management has always stressed such things as making production quotas and getting reports in on time, but hasn't given equal attention to the people side of the business.

To change the supervisors in an organization into first-class people managers requires the direct involvement of people at the top. When the big boss says, "The people in this organization are its greatest assets, and we're going to create the kind of work environment that will bring out the best in them," things begin to happen.

Of course, supervisors have to back up changed attitudes with action, and most of them have not been very good at relating with people, because they haven't learned how. In the past, this wasn't a recognized part of their job. There were few measures of how well they did it and few special rewards for doing it well.

If management is serious about its people and their productivity, it will have to retrain its supervisors and change their job descriptions. The training seminars we endorse are the result of top management's resolve to do this. After a few sessions, supervisors begin to realize that effective people relationships allow them to make quotas, and keep the machines running.

Your organization may have reached the point where it is ready to support a worker empowerment supervisory training program. Even without a program, however, you can move on your own. **You can start with this book.**

In the next chapter, we'll be talking about various kinds of organizations. You'll see an example of one supervisor in a poorly-managed organization where employee attitudes were at rock bottom. Yet he was able to lead his work group in a way that made them feel mile-high. Their performance was so outstanding that a university made a study of how they did it. The supervisor became a star. So can you.

5

TURN-ONS AND TURN-OFFS

Companies, non-profit institutions and government organizations can be autocratic, bureaucratic or any other kind of "atic," but within each one, you'll always find some bosses who are better than others at managing people.

Great supervisors are occasionally found in the worst organizations. A large eastern hospital commissioned researchers from the University of Chicago to find out what was wrong with its organization, which was having trouble serving physicians on its staff and patients to their satisfaction.

An employee attitude survey revealed that all departments of the hospital except one were far below norms in other hospitals in such things as how employees felt about their jobs and their bosses, satisfaction with the way grievances were handled, trust in management and pride in their work. The lone exception was the food service department, which not only stood out above other departments in the same hospital, but was at the top of the scale for hospital employees generally.

THE FOOD SERVICE MANAGER

Jobs in food service are not considered the most desirable in the hospital, and you'd expect to find the lower employee attitudes there. But in this food service department, employees liked their jobs and their boss, felt they

13

were providing a good product for the hospital and that it was a good place to work.

An in-depth study of the food service department disclosed that its manager had learned his trade in a New York restaurant under a chef who was a stickler for perfection. The chef tasted every dish prepared by his cooks, each of whom he held strictly accountable for quality. Kitchen employees gathered around for each tasting, waiting for his judgment -- a nod of approval, or rejection if the soup or sauce fell short of his high standard.

In the hospital kitchen, the manager followed the chef's example as he undertook to revitalize the failing food service. Doctors had been complaining that their instructions for patient diets were not followed accurately, and patients found their food trays unappetizing. Other hospital employees belittled kitchen workers, and their morale was low.

WHAT HE DID RIGHT

The new manager was **tough** on shortcomings, but **considerate** of his people. He got them to set high standards for themselves, then held them rigorously to meeting those standards. Like his mentor, the restaurant chef, he used showmanship. For example, he had his staff prepare a gourmet dinner for a doctors' meeting, allowing each cook to use creativity with a special dish, which he sampled. The feast was a sensation among the doctors and proved to be a turning point in their relations with the food service department. Patient trays were tastefully presented with a fresh flower and delivered hot. Each diet was painstakingly prepared as prescribed.

The manager instilled pride by demanding and getting the best from each worker. Interviews by the research team showed that workers regarded their boss as stern but kind -- a leader who knew them personally, looked out for their interests and gave them compliments, but only when

they deserved them. He made them feel that they were
important to the hospital, as indeed they were.

At another hospital in the Midwest, there were two
nursing units on the same floor. They were identical in
function, number of beds, number of staff and type of
patient. Yet an employee attitude survey showed that the
staffs of the two units had totally different views about
their working conditions, their pay, their futures and
whether the hospital was a good place to work.

TWO NURSING SUPERVISORS

One group felt good about themselves and their jobs;
the other did not. The only difference in the conditions
under which each group worked was in the way the two
nurse supervisors treated those under them. As
professional nurses, both supervisors were equally skilled.
They were equally competent as administrators. They
were about the same age and had the same length of
tenure at the hospital.

The sole difference between them was in how they
related to their staffs -- the way they talked to them,
listened to what they had to say, resolved their problems
and revealed their inner feelings through facial expression
and tone of voice.

The point of these two examples is that you, as a
supervisor, **create** a working environment, positive or
negative, by the way you treat your people. **The
environment will shape your people to make them
either upbeat and productive, or downcast, listless,
and mediocre.**

The food service manager inherited a group of workers
with little education and low status among the hospital

employees. His predecessor had treated them as "a bunch of dumb clucks," and they acted like dumb clucks. The new manager saw each one as a person with some potential that could be developed. He gave them a sense of worth, and they responded to his challenges.

The nurse supervisor who was cold and aloof inspired hostility among her nurses and got minimum performance from them in answer to her demands. The supervisor who was responsive and open made her nurses feel the same way, and their feelings shone through to help patients recover.

You have more power than you know over your people. It helps you become a good people manager, of course, if you have company policy and the whole organization behind you, **but you can do it on your own**, even if the front office doesn't care whether you exist. Moreover, you can learn to supervise effectively, **even if you feel it doesn't come naturally.** You can change your style that falls short for one that will work better for satisfying the people under you.

The next two chapters will give you some clues to understanding your people and what they're looking for from you to make them turn on to their full capacity. Then, we will give you some simple things you can do to meet both their needs and the expectations of your organization.

6

WHY PEOPLE ACT LIKE THAT

Who are these people you're supposed to supervise?

If they were just replaceable parts in the production process, it wouldn't make much difference who they are. If one wasn't working out, you'd get somebody else.

But people aren't machine parts. Before you go getting rid of one who doesn't fit just right, remember that each is a human being with a load of past experiences that have shaped the kind of person who is now your responsibility. Each also has a potential that you, as a boss, have the power to bring out.

Helping employees who are troubled to overcome their old hurts and hangups and become better adjusted, more successful and more productive is both a challenging and rewarding supervisory responsibility.

THE FOREMAN AND THE HIPPIE

This story of what one foreman in a large parking garage did with and for an 18-year old hippie type will help you understand how you go about reaching out to your people and helping them solve their problems.

When the lad in this actual case first came to work as a handyman in the parking garage, he had long, unkempt hair, wore tattered jeans and displayed a rebellious attitude that kept him just on the edge of being fired. He was showing up for work only four days a week. When asked how come, he said with a straight face that he came

17

in four days a week, because he just couldn't make it on his pay for three days!

Something about this young rebel intrigued his boss, who took the time to talk with him about his personal life -- how he was brought up, people he trusted or distrusted, his general outlook and what he was looking for. Little by little, he began to understand the young man. The boss found that underneath, he was more dissatisfied with himself than with his low level job or the world around him.

The boss didn't tell him to shape up or else, but did talk about the better jobs with the organization, where he could use his intelligence and build a career for himself. He told of some of the options and benefits available to employees, including a tuition refund for continuing education.

These ideas gradually began to sink in. One day, he came in with a haircut and wearing better clothes. He began arriving at work on time five days a week. Taking advantage of the tuition refund program, he enrolled in night college classes, eventually earning a two-year associate degree, then a bachelor's degree and finally a master's degree in counseling psychology.

A few years later, this young man said that without the acceptance and encouragement from his first boss, he would probably still be a drifter.

So you see, you can't always take people at their face value. Slovenly, careless attitudes, rebelliousness and sullen responses are not always due to resentment toward the job itself or toward you, but rather to some lingering feeling of having been cheated earlier in life, or perhaps some current problem that has nothing to do with work. People "act like that" for reasons that often seem mysterious.

You may not understand these reasons, but you can show that you care and set them on the way toward solving their own problems.

DEALING WITH PERSONAL TRAGEDIES

A supervisor in a large health care center told of her experience while she was still a staff nurse. A serious tragedy in her family had devastated her so much that she had trouble keeping her mind on her work. She could hardly function and wondered whether she would survive.

Luckily, she had an understanding supervisor who knew the way to help her was not to reduce her work load, but to hold her to a normal pace while giving her some emotional support for the burden she was bearing. The nurse regained her mental and physical health and later earned a promotion to become a supervisor herself.

"If it hadn't been for the rigor and discipline of the work and the understanding of my supervisor," she said, " I don't think I could have survived this traumatic time in my life."

RECOGNIZE THE HURTS

What lessons can you draw from these two examples? First, you can begin to look at troubled or troublesome employees as **basically good people with hurts.** You'll always have to test this assumption, of course, and you may find a few genuinely bad apples, but it's the best point of view from which to start.

Next, you can dismiss the idea that a "rest cure" is the right treatment to help people get over their hurts. In fact, some problems grow worse when people don't have enough to do. In times of emotional crisis, they need a structure to hang onto, and this is what the work environment provides. **Being part of a business unit that is functioning well brings recognition, a sense of security and a feeling that life is under control.** Taking responsibility as part of a team is stimulating. It keeps the mental processes active. These are the medicines that heal emotional hurts.

YOU CREATE THE ENVIRONMENT

The supervisor plays the leading role in creating this positive and healthy work environment that workers know they can count on day after day.

Firm and consistent leadership is what everyone looks for in the boss. Even if you can't erase memories of injuries and injustices or alter intolerable difficulties at home, the work environment you create by your words and actions can be a haven where **hurts have a chance to heal and life can get back on track.**

Bosses sometimes have a hard time accepting these ideas. They are usually the ones who learned to supervise by following the example of their bosses, most of whom believed you had to "treat 'em rough" to get the work out.

Don't get the impression that you should be "soft" on misbehavior. You have to confront it. If people with hurts are allowed to coast, their condition deteriorates and demoralizes co-workers, who see they are not pulling a full load. What you are learning is a more effective way than an old-fashioned dressing down to deal with such people.

If you doubt there are many workers in industry requiring individual attention, recent studies show that more than half of American homes are what we call "dysfunctional." That means children are being raised in families where violence, neglect, mistrust, alcoholism or drugs are common. These things leave a mark, but do not necessarily destroy good qualities that you can help the person discover and develop. Industry can't afford to overlook such cases or toss them back on society. **The turnaround potential is with you,** the first-line supervisors of America.

7

THE BIG THREE PEOPLE SKILLS

Of the three items below, which do you think is the most important in your job as a supervisor?

_____ **Technical knowledge**

_____ **Administrative ability**

_____ **Skill in handling people**

That was a trick question, because in modern management thinking, **all three** are of equal importance. It's true that in the past most first-line supervisors were chosen for their technical knowledge and work skills. Once on the job, they quickly learned their paperwork and how to submit their reports. Much less attention was given to how they treated people or how those under them reacted.

All this has changed. As productivity became a big issue, relations between supervisors and workers grew in importance. Unfortunately, most supervisors today are still not picked for their people skills or trained to acquire them. The next several chapters will give you the **three basic things** you need to know and be able to do in order to be an effective people manager. Their names may be unfamiliar to you, but you'll have no trouble understanding what they mean.

The first we call **Interacting.** Quite simply, this means talking and listening to others and recognizing their individual worth. As a supervisor, you should try to do this every day with each person under you. What you talk about is not particularly important, but it should be something **within the worker's field of interest.** It needn't have anything to do with work. "How's your son's broken leg?" or "How do you like your new lawn mower?" will do. Anything can be a starter. The reason for Interacting is that this is how you recognize people. It shows you care about them, that the things they do are of importance to you.

The second practice is called **Confronting,** a word that sounds worse than it is. It really means making people reason, bringing their attention to something that's important and getting them to say what they intend to do about it. Confronting is useful in dealing with errors or disruptive behavior, and it has its positive side. For example, if someone has been worried about some personal problem, you can help by getting the person to confront the issue, think up possible ways to solve it and make a choice among the options available for its solution. Confronting always moves through three stages that will be discussed in a later chapter.

The third skill you'll have to master is **Decision Sharing,** which involves letting loose of some of your power and giving your people a say in how their work is to be done. You don't need to fear this will undermine your authority. You'll come out stronger than ever and be freed for more important things than handling a welter of details your workers can handle for themselves. Decision Sharing is very difficult for some bosses until they learn how to do it as shown in Chapters 16 and 17.

These three people practices -- **Interacting, Confronting** and **Decision Sharing** -- work together to create a positive and healthy environment for your team to turn in its top performance. Everyone will benefit.

8

WHY AND HOW TO TALK
WITH YOUR PEOPLE

This chapter is about the first of the Big Three people practices -- **Interacting**, or talking, listening and showing interest in your workers. Why is this so important?

Think about what it's like to be a worker instead of a boss. You are at the bottom of the totem pole. You have no power in the organization. You do what you have to do to get through the shift. Somebody else tells you what to do and how to do it. Is it any wonder so many workers develop a "What the heck" attitude?

It's different for you as a boss. You go to important supervisor meetings. You have conversations with higher-ups in your organization. Your workers know who you are, but do you know who they are? Here's a real-life example that points up the difference between being a worker and being a boss.

After seven years on the job, a skilled worker was promoted to supervisor. The first morning he came to work after his promotion, four co-workers greeted him with, "Good morning, Bob."

"That was four more 'Good mornings' than I received in the last two weeks," he said. Suddenly, he was a somebody.

Workers know how much depends on getting along with the boss. They may like you or hate you, but in either case, you are important to them and they follow what you do. If you like football, then they'd better like football, as this example from a large machine tool shop shows.

Two foremen in the shop had season tickets to the Chicago Bears' home games. They also traveled to see out-of-town games. Among workers in their groups, the supervisors' presence at the games was the subject of daily conversation. They commented on games just played and those coming up, where the bosses' seats were located and where they'd be staying on weekend trips. What the supervisors did was of importance to them. Sure, it made the supervisors feel important.

But what workers do in their spare time is rarely of much interest to anyone, especially to the boss. The work day passes without a sign of personal recognition. Each worker is just a cog in the wheels of production. Nothing to distinguish one working stiff from another. The cold, impersonal nature of the average job is reflected in the apathy of the workers and the mediocrity of their performance. There is little to make them feel important.

MAKING THEM FEEL LIKE SOMEBODY

Supervisors have it in their power to make their workers feel they are somebody, if they will just take the time to call them by name and start a short conversation. Recognition by the boss can give a worker who feels put down and inferior a sense of self-worth and vitality. Job performance turns from humdrum to turned-on. This chemistry takes place because of the supervisor's position. It's not just anybody talking. It's the boss!

Being a nobody hurts. Those who feel small often try to get rid of the pain by calling attention to themselves through bullying, bragging, outlandish clothes or hairdos, or acting sick or helpless. The TV character, Ralph Kramden, played by Jackie Gleason, made a fool of himself by pretending to be a big shot. Carroll O'Connor's Archie Bunker shielded his hurts with bigotry and wound up being ridiculous whenever his bluff was called.

The skilled supervisor treats these hurts by seeing beyond the disguises and recognizing the individual as someone who really is worthy of attention. The process of talking, rather than the specifics of what is said, provides the healing. Left unattended or aggravated in the workplace, the hurts that so many people bring to work will fester and cause trouble in the form of disruptive behavior and substandard performance.

Under the right kind of boss, mixed up workers have a chance to stop being defensive and start living a better kind of life.

Great for them, but what about you? It takes time and effort to develop interacting skills, and there ought to be some reward for supervisors who do it. There is. After you have helped someone, it is rewarding to watch the person mature and grow. Beyond that, there are byproducts that make a supervisor's job a lot easier.

Workers to whom you have given a sense of self-worth and importance are in a positive frame of mind. They will respect you for knowing and doing your job, just as you respect them for what they are. They will no longer try to "one up" you and make your day a bummer, but will be glad to be on your team and will do their best to help it win.

You'll find that the responses you get from positive interacting give a boost to your day. A workplace with a pleasant hum buoys up everybody, including you, the supervisor.

GENUINE TALK

How do you talk in a genuine way that tells the worker, "You're somebody?" You first have to find things of interest to the worker, so that your conversation focuses on the employee rather than yourself. You start talking with some general question or comment, such as "How's it going, Flo?" Flo answers. Now you respond to whatever she says, which will be in her area of interest and mood at the moment. The conversation continues in her world until it reaches a natural ending. It need not run long.

As a supervisor, **employee - focused** interaction proceeds in three steps:

1. You **open** the conversation.
2. You **listen** to how they respond.
3. You **respond** to their **response.**

Suppose when you ask Flo, "How's it going?" she says "Not good. My daughter's asthma is acting up again."

Your next comment is about her daughter's condition and what care is available to her, or about Flo's feelings at the moment. You show that what's happening to her is important enough to deserve your attention. You don't dismiss it with, "That's too bad, Flo. Have a nice day," a sure sign of a phony concern.

This kind of interacting must be initiated by the supervisor. Subordinates feel in no position to open a conversation with the boss on anything not related to the job. They won't stick their necks out, partly because they fear their superior may rebuff them, but more because they fear censure by their peers for brown nosing or being pushy.

It's hard for some supervisors to break away from old stereotypes of what it means to be a boss. The Army used to teach officers that it was wrong to fraternize with the troops. Control was all-important. Officers had to be sure of unquestioning obedience when they ordered soldiers into battle.

The military notion that there are two kinds of people -- officers and enlisted -- somehow carried over into the business world. Managers were told not to get too close to rank and file employees, or they wouldn't be able to maintain discipline. Nonsense. Today, we know how supervisors **can keep control and still show a genuine interest in their subordinates.** By developing and practicing new people-relating skills, breaking with the past becomes easier.

THE FENDER BENDERS

Change in the way supervisors talk with their subordinates is taking place throughout industry. A soft drink company in a large metropolitan area was having an unusual number of fender-bending accidents with its trucks. The cost of repairs was showing up on the company's bottom line, leading top management to look into the trouble. A consultant brought in to look into it interviewed a number of the drivers and their supervisors and rode in the trucks on their delivery routes.

After some weeks, he reported to management: "You think more of your trucks than you do of your people. Every day, when the trucks return to the garage, they are carefully washed, any necessary repairs are made, tire pressures are checked, they are loaded with products to be delivered the next day, and lined up for the morning drive-out.

"At about 6 A.M., the drivers arrive at a bull pen to get their route sheets for the day. No one says 'Good Morning' or asks how things are going. The managers come in to issue orders. The drivers get in their trucks and drive off with hardly a word from their bosses to cheer their day."

"So what?" said the supervisors. "These are union guys who make good money. What more do they want?"

"They want some recognition that they're important to the company. Besides driving the trucks, they're almost your only contact with the customers. They sell and service the stores. They would like some show of appreciation that the kind of job they do makes a difference. They're not getting it. The fender benders are their way of calling attention to the fact."

What was the remedy? The managers started a new morning ritual of having coffee with the drivers for about 15 minutes before the drivers took off. They shot the bull with them and listened to any problems the drivers might want to get off their chests. In other words, they **interacted.** The number of fender benders declined almost immediately. It was the start of a new day in driver-boss relationships.

How you connect with each subordinate determines how each feels about self, the job and the company. You can give your workers a feeling of worth and power, or you can push them down, just by the way you talk, or don't talk. They'll interpret silence as indifference, telling them you have more important things to do than to talk to them. It doesn't take a lot of words or a big chunk of your time to make a world of difference to your workers. Try it.

MAKING THE CONNECTION

It can be as simple as making eye contact and nodding with a smile. It's not always necessary to say something. The fact that you notice the employee is enough to make a positive connection. Doing this requires no extra time or effort on your part. You're walking down the aisle anyway.

The next step up is to say something like "How y'a doing, Bob?" The response may be no more than "Fine, thanks," as you walk past, but you've recognized and shown interest in the employee.

Following are six examples, drawn from factories and offices, of interacting in more depth. In each case, the supervisor finds a topic of interest to the worker to talk about.

THE CORNFIELD

SUPV: Hi John. Did your corn survive the hail storm?

JOHN: Fairly well. We got some damage to the upper leaves, but it hasn't tasseled out yet. So I think it will be all right.

SUPV: You have insurance, don't you?

JOHN: Yes, but I don't think it will kick in.

SUPV: Could have been worse. East of town seems to have been hit more.

JOHN: That's true.

THE KIDS

SUPV: Hi Mary. I see where your daughter won a ribbon in the horse show.

MARY: She sure did. And in a pretty big field.

SUPV: Is she riding a new horse this year?

MARY: Yes, and he's going to get better as Judy keeps working with him.

SUPV: How often does she ride?

MARY: Just about every day now.

SUPV: She's quite a gal.

MARY: She sure is.

THE ROCK GROUP

SUPV: Hey Joe! Did you join a new rock group? My son Bob said he saw you with the Space Blasters last night.

JOE: Naw. I was just filling in for one of their guys.

SUPV: Bob said they featured you a lot.

JOE: Yeah, they did.

SUPV: You sure have talent. You do a lot of things well.

JOE: Thanks. I try.

SUPV: Well, it sure shows.

JOE: Thanks again.

BAD BACK

SUPV: How's that back these days, Bob?

BOB: Some days fine. Some not so good.

SUPV: Still going for rehab?

BOB: Three nights a week.

SUPV: What do they say?

BOB: Just keep it up. They're trying to strengthen the abdominal muscles. I guess they have a lot to do with the lumbar region where my injury was.

SUPV: You're kidding. You mean your stomach muscles support your back?

BOB: So they tell me. I believe it, too. I notice quite a difference now that I'm toughening up the old gut. Lost about 15 pounds down there. I was pretty discouraged for a while, but now I think I'm going to make it.

SUPV: I admire your courage, Bob. Keep at it.

BASEBALL

SUPV: Hi Pete. What do you think of those Cubbies now?

PETE: Some days I own 'em. Some days I don't. Their fielding is OK and their pitching is holding up, but they can't seem to get any consistent hitting. That tail end of the batting order is killing us.

SUPV: They're running a lot of different players in the lineup.

PETE: Yeah, but it doesn't help. They've paid too much for the wrong players.

SUPV: Oh well, maybe next year.

PETE: Yeah, always next year. I grew up with that.

SUPV: Some day, Pete.

PETE: Yeah! Some day.

THE JOB

SUPV: Hi Joan. Haven't seen you for awhile.

JOAN: Oh I've been here, all right. Chasing around all over the place trying to keep those new copying machines running.

SUPV: What's wrong with them?

JOAN: Nothing really wrong with the machines. It's just that people haven't learned how to use them.

31

They're always getting paper fouled up in the works. They try to fix it themselves and that only makes it worse.

SUPV: We're lucky to have you around to keep us going.

JOAN: Yes, well, I kind of enjoy keeping busy.

SUPV: You're doing a good job, and a lot of people appreciate it.

Note in these interactions that all were initiated by the supervisor. In each, the supervisor picked up on the worker's response. The supervisor always enhanced the worker's sense of self-worth and left the worker in a positive frame of mind at the end of the conversation. None of these interactions took more than about ten seconds, and some took even less. What seems like small talk answers a basic need and serves a good purpose.

DON'T FORGET "GOOD MORNING"

The supervisor who fails to say "Good morning" to an assistant can trigger a chain of worries in the assistant's mind. One supervisor unthinkingly walked past her assistant's desk without a word and entered her office. Shortly after, there was a quiet knock on her door.

"Are you mad at me? Did I do something wrong?" the assistant asked fearfully.

Startled, the supervisor said, "No! What gave you that idea?"

"You walked right by my desk with your head down and didn't say 'Good morning'. I thought for sure I was in some kind of trouble."

"I'm so sorry," the supervisor said. "I wasn't even aware of it, I was so wrapped up in something that's come up, I was just not thinking."

This shows how important you are to the people under you and how their lives are affected by the things you say and do.

Most supervisors who hadn't been in the habit of saying "Good morning" or "shooting the breeze" are surprised at the good things that happen when they try it.

Albert was a technically-minded supervisor in a large medical center. He was somewhat bashful and had to be pushed to interact with members of his staff.

After several weeks of practice, he commented: "It was a real chore at first. It wasn't in my nature. But after a while, I was getting such good response I actually enjoyed it. I learned things about each member of my staff that enabled me to have a real dialogue with them. Interacting opened up a lot in our department and made our unit more productive. It also opened me up a lot. I endorse it."

9

LEVELING WITH PEOPLE

Now to the second of the Big Three people practices --
Confronting. Let's assume you are a boss and you have a
boss. How do you react when your boss --

1. Chews you out for a mistake.

2. Pussyfoots around an issue, leaving you wondering
   what's wrong.

3. Ignores issues, hoping they'll go away.

4. Seldom notices the good things you do or gives you
   compliment.

5. Levels with you at all times, telling you plainly
   when you've made a mistake and praising you
   when you deserve it.

You probably resent the first four kinds of treatment
and welcome the last. You'll go all out for a boss who is
square with you and treats you like a grown up human
being. The people under you have the same feelings you
have. They may not have your experience or ability, but
they aren't dumb. They can think for themselves and
figure things out. **Part of your job as a supervisor is
not only to let them think, but to see that they do.**
That's the only way you can bring out the best that's in
them and raise the performance of your group.

Leveling with people opens the way to a genuine, two-
way discussion on any subject. If you habitually order
them around or put them down, they'll come to accept this
as the way you operate and will find ways to survive.
They'll clam up on you, talk behind your back and do
enough work to get by, but they won't give you any more
than they have to.

With a level playing field, you can meet your workers face to face on issues that continually crop up in any plant or office. This is where you settle issues intelligently in a way that is good for your workers and for you. You can confront issues squarely without old-fashioned bossism that leaves bruised feelings and hidden resentments that lead to retaliation in one form or another.

This approach is called **constructive confronting**. As you learn to use it, you'll find it helps you in many ways. It invites your workers to cooperate with you instead of balking and fighting you. It gives them a part in how issues are resolved. It draws out their savvy about the job and gets new ideas on the table. In time, they'll volunteer suggestions for improvements. You won't have to come up with every new idea yourself.

Getting your workers to think straight and see beyond their own interests helps them grow up. Everybody has a two-sided nature. This new type of confronting brings out the **responsible** side rather than the **evasive, uncooperative** side.

Constructive confronting differs from old-fashioned confronting, which tells subordinates what to do with a voice of authority. When you confront constructively, you involve the worker as a responsible partner. You speak in a calm, conversational voice. You ask questions and expect responsible answers. You seek different ways to solve a problem and weigh each suggestion to find the best way, no matter where it comes from. You end every encounter on a positive note. You wipe the slate clean and start out fresh for whatever comes up next.

As you learn to confront constructively, you'll find it takes a lot of grief off your mind. Your headaches will cure themselves, because workers will be taking responsibility for their own problems. You'll have time to spend on more creative parts of your job -- keeping up on technology, devising better systems and strengthening ties with the rest of your organization. **Instead of putting out fires, you can devote your time to fireproofing.**

10

HOW TO CONFRONT CONSTRUCTIVELY

Constructive confronting has a set process that moves through three stages. These stages are:

1. **OPENING.** This has two parts:

    a. **Present the issue.**

    b. **Reach agreement** with the worker that the issue exists.

2. **PROBLEM SOLVING.** This also has two parts:

    a. **Get the worker to take the lead** in solving the issue.

    b. **Get the issue settled** one way or another.

3. **CLOSING.** End on a positive note.

Eight Essentials to Learn

To become a successful confronter, you must understand and do the following:

1. **Know where you're going.** Recognize the three stages of confrontation and be aware of what stage you're in as you move through them.

2. **State the opening issue clearly and directly** in a way that encourages an open-minded response from the worker.

3. **Speak in a normal, conversational tone of voice.**

4. **Draw out the worker's views** on how an issue is to be resolved.

5. **Develop several solutions to the problem.**

6. **Involve the worker in selecting which solution is best,** without giving up right of final choice.

7. **When solution has been decided, close on a positive note.**

8. For important or complex issues, **make a written record of action to be taken by all parties** as a reference point for the future.

The first point listed above, **know where you're going,** applies to the three stages -- Opening, Problem Solving, and Closing. These stages are your road map, so that you always know "where you're at." They provide the logical framework for dealing with any issue, keeping you from getting thrown off track by side issues as the discussion heats up.

You control the confrontation by moving with determination through the three stages, knowing that you won't be able to reach the next stage until you've finished the one before it.

The other seven points apply in varying degree to one or more of the three stages. Some take longer to complete than others, but all are important. The next chapter takes up the second point -- **stating the issue.** You need to know how to do this effectively in the opening stage of constructive confronting.

11

STATING THE ISSUE

Before you confront your worker, think through what the issue is, then write it out in clear, direct terms. Present it forthrightly and **determine whether the worker recognizes it as a real issue.** If you don't get this recognition at the outset, you can't move to the problem solving stage, because the worker won't be a party to the solution.

The discussion then focuses on getting agreement that there is an issue. It may take some time just to reach the second stage, problem solving.

Here are three cases of the sort you might encounter. What kind of opening statement would you make to confront the worker? Use the lines below each case to write your statement, keeping it direct and concise, leaving no doubt as to the issue, yet creating an atmosphere where the worker can think clearly. Then compare your statements with our suggested examples at the end of each case.

CASE #1

A window manufacturer has a procedure for workers to sign out tools they take from the tool crib and sign them in when returned. John has been taking tools out without recording them on the master sheet. He always returns them, but other workers have noted him ignoring the procedure and called your attention to it.

You have observed him doing this twice in the last three days. You are about to call him into your office to confront him about it. On the lines below, or on a separate sheet of paper, write out how you would open the confrontation.

_____

_____

_____

_____

_____

Suggested opening for case #1

"John, we have a procedure for signing out and signing in tools you take from the crib. In the last three days, I've seen you ignore this procedure two times. What do you think you can do to follow the procedure in the future?"

Comment: This opening is direct and to the point. It leaves the worker with a clear head to figure out his problem.

CASE #2

You observed Jean, a registered nurse, rudely telling family members who had stayed in a patient's room after the hospital's visiting hours, "You people know when visiting hours are up. I want all of you to get out of here now!"

This kind of abruptness goes against the hospital's policy of being considerate to patients and visitors alike. Shortly after, you are about to confront Jean on her behavior. Write out your opening statement below.

_____

_____

_____

_____

Suggested opening for case #2

"Jean, the way you told the family of the girl in Room 16 to leave after visiting hours didn't match up with our policy of consideration for visitors. How aware are you of the policy, and to what degree did you violate it?"

Comment: This statement is direct and concise. It starts the confrontation by giving Jean a chance to measure her own behavior against hospital policy.

CASE #3

Buck is a maintenance plumber in headquarters of a large insurance company. June is a young cleaning woman in the maintenance department. You happened to overhear Buck tell her, "Your fanny sure looks good when you swing that broom."

She said, "Knock it off. Enough's enough," but he followed up with , "Come on, now. You swing that fanny just for me, you know that.

Buck was accused by a co-worker once before of sexual harassment but was not reprimanded for it. You are going to confront him. Write out your opening statement.

_____

_____

_____

_____

Suggested opening for case #3

"Buck, I overheard your hallway talk to June this morning. You crossed the line between good-natured kidding and sexual harassment. June's reaction indicated she was offended when she told you, 'Enough's enough,' but you didn't stop. To what degree are you aware that you crossed the line?"

Comment. This approach opens the door for Buck to start examining the effect his sexual remarks have on women. The Bucks of this world have to learn what harassing does to people. Constructive confronting forces him to face his own behavior and grow up.

Opening statements are crucial to getting a confrontation off on the right foot. You have to get the issue **defined** and put the other person in a **frame of mind** to be willing and able to think through the problem sensibly.

You keep the discussion on track by sticking to the main issue when side issues or irrelevancies are brought up. Constructive confronting is not designed to punish or humiliate, but to show concern and help people develop their better sides, while solving a problem at the same time.

We'll return to these three examples to see what happens in the **problem-solving** stage of confrontation, but first, let's look beyond the words you use to state the issue. The way you say those words may have more to do than the words themselves with how your worker receives them.

12

TONE OF VOICE
TELLS THE TRUTH

The sound of your voice, as much as the words you use, tell your listener what you're really thinking as you speak. In the chapter on stating the issue, you learned the importance of putting your worker in a reasoning frame of mind where a discussion between you can proceed to a logical solution. If the tone of your voice suggests that you are angry, hostile or reprimanding, you will get a defensive response that closes the door to logical thinking.

What the worker hears you say sets the stage, and what is heard is not always what you intended to say. You can say the same thing in various tones of voice, stressing different words or syllables, and be saying something different each time.

How many twists can you give to this question: **"What did you do that for?"** As you will probably discover, the meaning of the question changes when you change the emphasis on the words.

"What **did** you do that for?" says you think the employee made a mistake and you're pretty mad about it.

"What did **you** do that for?" points the finger at one employee who is out of line with the rest of the group.

"What did you **do** that for?" like the first example, implies a foregone conclusion, but with even more anger and impatience with the employee.

"What did you do **that** for?" is less threatening than the three above, but expresses mystification as to the reason for the employee's action.

"What did you do that **for?**" tells the employee you think there may be a reason for the action and you'd like to know what it is.

"What did you do that for?" in an even tone of voice without stress on any word in particular displays a calm, impartial attitude and genuine desire for information. It is entirely non-threatening and gets a rational response in almost any interchange.

Self-control in how you think and feel lies behind control of your voice. It is hard to disguise anger, prejudice, impatience, displeasure and other negative inner feelings. Instead of trying to submerge these emotions and make your voice sound like something you are not, start working with the thought processes that generate feelings and determine how people talk, act and react.

THE TA SYSTEM

Some years ago, a psychiatrist named Berne developed the theory that our thoughts at any time are running in one of three channels, which he called the Parent, the Child and the Adult. We speak and act differently, depending on the channel we are in at the moment. To a large extent, we can control which **channel** to use.

As we think, so we feel and so we act. This is the basis of the system called Transactional Analysis, or TA for short, which Dr. Berne laid out to help people deal and communicate effectively with each other.

When you think and act like a parent, you treat others as if they were children. You tell them what to do. You put on superior airs that say in effect, "I'm better than you are, and I know what's best." You may use punishment to get what you want, but you can also be kind and protective, as parents often are.

Acting and talking like a parent to your subordinates makes them feel like children, and you can expect them to respond as a child would respond. When their minds are in the child channel, people react to the parent in one of three ways -- through rebellion, submission or evasion. The rebellious child may fight you or turn sullen, secretly planning a way to get back at you later. The submissive child will adapt to whatever you say, but won't take any initiative. The evasive child, which Berne calls "L'il Professor," will seek ways to get around you and may be good at "one uping you."

There are times when the good qualities of childhood that stay with us as we grow older can be very useful and should be encouraged. The natural child in us is imaginative, inventive and uninhibited -- just what you need when looking for new ideas. Light-hearted humor and merriment are also child-like in origin and can help relieve the monotony of a routine work day, as long as they don't get out of hand.

When you're talking like a parent to someone, the reaction you get will depend on what **kind** of parent you sound like. Dr. Berne identified three parent types -- **critical parent, demon/witch parent and nurturing parent.** The words you use and the tone of your voice tell which kind you are.

Critical Parent

The critical parent in you orders others about, accuses, blames, knows what's best, has no confidence in the ability of others. Listen to yourself and listen to others to hear the critical parent speaking:

"You know better than that. This line has to keep running. Start using your head."

"Can't you do anything right? Here, give me that wrench and I'll fix it."

"If I've told you once, I've told you ten times."

Demon/Witch

The worst type of parent is the demon/witch -- the hollering, humiliating, bullying kind of supervisor who strikes terror into underlings and relies on fear to get the job done. Here are some typical demon/witch harangues:

"I'll have you out of here if you don't pay more attention to what you're doing."

"Look, Buster! It's my way or the highway. And I'll promise you -- you won't ever work anywhere in this industry again."

"You're not paid to think. Do as you're told. I'll show you who's in charge. I'll pound some sense into that thick head of yours."

Nurturing Parent

There are times when some workers need the nurturing parent for protection and comfort. Don't hold back when you see this need. Do what you can to help the worker who's having trouble on the job, but don't prolong your nurturing to the point of dependency. Over-protective parents won't let their children grow up. Wise parents encourage them to stand on their own. When the need for parenting is past, let it go. Here's the way the nurturing parent talks:

"Ted, I know things aren't going well for you today. I think you ought to stand up a bit and stretch. You can do this job well. Try it again."

"Tom, you're one of the best workers we have. You just had tough luck in making that part. Sharpen your tool and make another one. I know you can do it."

"Jane, you did a great job on that report. I knew you could do it. You're catching on real well."

The Logical Adult

Parent talk should be used as little as possible at work. Try not to let the **critical** parent get into the act even if other measures have failed. Use the **nurturing** parent only when you see a real need for supportive encouragement, and never let the **demon/witch** come into the workplace.

Most of the time, you should be thinking and talking in the **adult** channel. When you are in this frame of mind, your subordinates will hear you as a leader they can trust, because you are consistently genuine and honest with them and caring about what they think.

Your tone of voice will have none of the preachiness or "Now hear this" of the parent, but will have an intelligent ring to it. In the adult channel, you are dealing in reality, with things as they are. You speak directly to the point, stating facts without blaming, accusing or making snide remarks. Just business-like, straightforward talk about the issue at hand.

This kind of adult talk pulls the listener into their adult channel, whereas parent talk forces the other person into the child. When you have engaged the responsible, reasoning side of your workers, they will come forward with initiatives that can lift your unit's performance and productivity. **This is the supervisor's reward for learning to use the TA system.**

VOICE CONTROL TAKES PRACTICE

Voice control is particularly important when you confront a subordinate in an effort to get at a problem, but it also plays a part in everyday interacting with your workers. Your voice tone can be cold or warm. It can make your words sound sincere or shallow.

Some people have trouble matching up their tone of voice with what they intend to say. That's why there are so many poor speakers who have to read their speeches to bored audiences.

Actors and singers seem to have natural control over their voices, but all of them have worked at it. It may take some practice on your part to acquire the voice skills you need to match the quality of the thought behind your words.

One useful exercise is paired sentences. Try reading the statements below. Each **first** sentence is a positive, pleasant statement, such as you might make to a worker in the ordinary course of a day. The **second** might be the opening of a confrontation. It is possible to keep a **parental** tone out of your voice when you are accusing someone, by thinking of the issue in adult terms. In this way you can avoid hostility and set the stage for a reasonable discussion.

If you have access to a tape recorder, it's a good idea to record your voice, then listen to it to hear how you sound. You might play it back for a friend, without telling what you were up to. Ask the listener what kind of mood you were in when you read each sentence. Try practicing on the following pairs:

A. Good job setting up for that special part this morning. You sure know that machine.

B. Why did you get so mad talking with the cost accountant yesterday? It didn't do us any good in the front office.

A. I left your car in the parking lot at pole 7. You've got a nice car there.

B. Why aren't you wearing your safety glasses? It's required throughout the whole area of operations.

A. We missed you during your vacation. I hope you enjoyed back-packing,

B. You put me in a bind with engineering with your

overdue report. Why can't you get it in on time?

A. Those signs you painted for the convention were first-rate. I didn't know you had all that talent.

B. Why are you giving customers such a hard time when you handle their complaints?

A. Tom's coming by tomorrow to pick up those castings. Say hello to him for me. I like that guy.

B. Your work area here is really a mess. It needs to be kept orderly. Is that clear to you?

A. That computer program you set up for us is working fine. You got our needs right.

B. How come you told me Friday you were going to make a three o'clock sales call on Gentry, and Joe sees you on the golf course at 2:30? What is this?

A. While you're over at the box factory, Jan is holding an order for us. Can you pick it up?

B. This is the third time we've talked about your passing confidential information. Do you know how serious this is? Why do you do it?

After you get the hang of it, write out some pairs of sentences built around situations you typically encounter on your own job, then read them as you did those above. These exercises show you that we do use different tones of voice for complimentary or neutral statements and for accusatory statements. The objective is to keep your voice in a conversational tone as far as possible, even when you have some cause to feel irritated.

So far, we've seen how to open a confrontation by stating the issue, the thought channel you should put yourself in before you do it, and the tone of voice you should try to maintain in addressing a worker. In the next chapter, we'll move on to the problem-solving stage of a confrontation.

13

SOLVING THE PROBLEM

In Chapter 11, you got some practice **stating** the issue in the opening stage of confrontation. Take a moment to review the statements you wrote out for the three work situations we presented and compare them again with the openings suggested.

Now you're ready to move on to the second stage of the confrontation, which involves getting your worker to take the lead as much as possible in **solving** the issue at hand. We'll start by continuing with Stage 2 in Case #1:

SIGNING OUT TOOLS

The problem as defined in Stage 1 was John's failure to follow plant procedures in signing out tools he borrows from the crib.   After you confronted John in the opening stage with the fact that he had been ignoring the sign out rules, we suggested that you ask him, "What do you think you can do to follow the procedure in the future?" From that point on, the problem solving stage might go something like this:

JOHN: It's a silly rule. Can anybody explain to me why I have to set the tool down and write my name and the time of the shift every time I take out a drill? That takes time and slows me down. Don't they trust me with a beat up tool that doesn't work half the time anyway?

SUPV: John, is it really the time it takes that's important to you, or your feeling that you're not trusted?

51

JOHN: Some of both. But more the lack of trust.
          Do they think I'm going to steal the cotton
          pickin' thing?

SUPV: Well, you know sometimes tools are lost. The
          system is a way of keeping track of where each
          tool is. But the main reasons for sign out and
          sign in are to find out how often tools are used
          and by what departments, and to know their
          condition, so they can be fixed or sharpened if
          need be. We don't have a full-time crib manager
          to check out the tools, so the master control sheet
          is our only way of knowing where tools are and
          what kind of shape they're in.

JOHN: Maybe so, but it just goes against my grain to
          have to stop and write down every single time I
          take out or bring back a tool.

SUPV: What do you think you can do to bring yourself to
          sign that master sheet? It's the procedure we use
          around here for the reasons I gave.

JOHN: I dunno. It's time consuming and insulting, too.

SUPV: But what do you think you can do to bring
          yourself to sign the master sheet?

JOHN: Well, I guess just sign the blooming thing.

SUPV: That's fine, John. Our unit is one of the best in
          the plant, and I appreciate your part in keeping it
          that way.

JOHN: Yeah, I know we're good . We all work hard.

SUPV: That's true, John. We do. So let's get on with it.

JOHN: Okay.

COMMENT: The first thing the supervisor did in
resolving the problem was to draw out John's feelings as to
why he didn't want to sign the tools out and back in. This
was the tip-off on the real reason John wasn't following the
procedure, and it also helped John get some resentment off
his chest. It gave the supervisor the chance to supply

information about the procedure that might let John change his mind without losing face. When John still stalled, the supervisor **repeated** the question like a broken record until John realized it was his shot to call. He finally concluded, "Well, I guess just sign the blooming thing."

If the supervisor had followed up with , "Well, you better," he would have made it an order and taken away John's responsibility for signing the sheet as a personal commitment. **Constructive confronting gets the worker to do what's right without being ordered.** It tells the worker: "You are a worthy and intelligent person who can think through how you ought to do your job. Now let's get on with it."

HOSPITAL POLICY

Now take the second case of the registered nurse who gave the patient's family a rough time in ordering them out after visiting hours were over. The supervisor confronted her on it by pointing out that her handling of the situation didn't match up with the hospital's policy of consideration for visitors. She asked Jean **how aware she was of the policy and to what degree she had violated it.** Picking up from that point, here's how Jean might be brought to solving the problem:

JEAN: Those people had been told fifteen minutes before that visiting hours were over.
Besides, can't they read signs? They're posted all over the hospital saying what the visiting hours are. Those people were just testing us to see if we'd throw them out. Well, I did.

SUPV: How aware are you, Jean, of the hospital policy of being considerate and polite to visitors?

JEAN: People like that deserve exactly what they get.

SUPV: Again Jean, how aware are you of the hospital policy?

JEAN:	Hospital policy, hospital policy! How aware are those folks of what they're doing to our work schedule? How can they expect us to take good care of their daughter when they're around?
SUPV:	Well then, how aware are you of the policy?
JEAN:	I'm fully aware of it. Why keep asking me?
SUPV:	To what extent do you think you violated it?
JEAN:	Not too much. Those people were violating hospital rules.
SUPV:	Do you think the policy applies sometimes, and sometimes it doesn't?
JEAN:	No, not really. A policy is a policy.
SUPV:	Why do you think we have a policy to be considerate and polite to visitors?
JEAN:	I suppose because they pay the bills. Be nice to our customers.
SUPV:	That's one reason for it, Jean. So to what extent do you think you violated the policy?
JEAN:	I guess quite a bit, but I did get them out of there.
SUPV:	That you did. In the future, how can you get them out of there and still be considerate and polite?
JEAN:	Hold my temper, I guess. You know I have a good one.
SUPV:	You do, Jean. And what might you do to hold your temper?
JEAN:	Bite my tongue, count to ten, zip my lip.
SUPV:	Well, you seem to have some choices.
JEAN:	Oh, I know what I have to do. I should have more poise, like you. I wish I had your skills that way.
SUPV:	Thank you, Jean. I've learned to zip my lip, as you say.

JEAN: I really do appreciate your patience in talking with me. I hope you'll keep it up. I know I'm a good nurse, even if I do overstep policy now and then.

SUPV: You are a good nurse, Jean. We'll keep working together and I'm sure you can learn how to handle people better.

JEAN: But Oh! If visitors would just stop testing me!

SUPV: Next time, I suspect they'll be put out with a smile, if my antenna is tuned right.

JEAN: I think it is.

SUPV: Okay, Jean.

COMMENT: Again, the double objective was to get Jean to face up to her rude behavior and think through how to correct it, and then to stop it without being ordered to do so. Her supervisor kept the initial discussion focused on how aware Jean was of the hospital policy, why it existed and to what extent she thought she had violated it. The supervisor's intent was not to threaten or punish, but to clarify and problem solve.

Jean at first defended her conduct, but when the supervisor persisted on the issue of whether Jean knew the policy and was aware that she had violated it, her good sense came to the fore and she correctly analyzed that it was her temper that triggered the rudeness. It then became a matter of getting Jean to decide how she would control her temper in similar situations.

Jean volunteered that she admired and wished she had her supervisor's poise and skills. This allowed the supervisor to affirm that the two would work together to develop Jean's ability to deal with people.

Jean got the message to stop being rude to visitors and also resolved to change herself by acquiring her supervisor's poise, again proving that constructive confronting is **teaching** as well as **correcting**.

SEXUALLY HARASSING REMARKS

Case #3 opened with the supervisor confronting Buck for making suggestive remarks to June, a young cleaning woman in the maintenance department. June told Buck to "Knock it off. Enough's enough." But Buck kept on and was overheard by his supervisor, who told him he had crossed the line between good natured kidding and sexual harassment and asked him, "To what degree are you aware that you crossed the line?" From that point, the problem solving stage went as follows:

BUCK: Aware of? I'm not aware of anything, because I didn't do anything. She wanted me to notice her. I can tell by watching. She gets everything in motion when she sweeps that broom.

SUPV: You think she moves her body more than she needs to when she sweeps the hallway, is that it?

BUCK: No, but Gosh, fella, that's enough. It was wiggling all over the place.

SUPV: Buck, how familiar are you with the new sexual harassment regulations?

BUCK: I went through that silly hour talk and movie personnel put on.

SUPV: What did that tell you?

BUCK: What I got out of it was don't touch, threaten or demand sex favors.

SUPV: What about making unwelcome remarks about a lady's body?

BUCK: Well yeah. But she was asking for my remarks. Welcoming them.

SUPV: Even when she said enough's enough?

BUCK: Aw, she didn't really mean it.

SUPV: How do you know?

BUCK: I can tell. I know that kind.

SUPV: That kind happens to be an employee who was

performing her assigned duty. She has a right to do her job without being ogled and harassed by a co-worker, particularly after she told you enough is enough. In the future, how do you think you can tell whether you're offending female employees with sexually-oriented remarks?

BUCK: I don't know.

SUPV: Think some more, Buck. How can you tell?

BUCK: Don't talk sexy talk to them. Whee! They're all so touchy these days.

SUPV: Let me review what personnel told us in that harassment meeting. First, our company has a policy prohibiting sexual harassment. Second, the offender as well as the company is at fault and liable if it occurs. Third, sexually suggestive remarks are a no no if they're intentional or repeated, unwanted or unreturned, or if they interfere with someone's ability to do a job, or if they create a hostile work environment for someone who's offended. They drilled us on these points and told us to get them down pat. What do they mean to you?

BUCK: They mean women can be sexy with us, but we can't be sexy with them.

SUPV: The way I heard it, it works both ways. Whether you make unwanted or offensive remarks to a woman or she makes them to you, those remarks in a workplace are illegal.

BUCK: Boy! Things are really changing. What next?

SUPV: I don't know, Buck, but this is one change you'd better make. Any doubt about that?

BUCK: No, you make it pretty clear.

SUPV: You understand how severe these harassment regulations are and what they consist of?

BUCK:	I do now.
SUPV:	I'd suggest you get out those materials from personnel and get those three points about company policy, liability and suggestive remarks burned into your mind. I did that myself, because we should all know them by heart. It's the law of the land.
BUCK:	Sure sounds like it's for real.
SUPV:	It is, Buck. And I'm glad you understand it now, because I'd hate to see you in any kind of trouble. Now let's get back to work.
BUCK:	Yeah. Let's get back to work. See ya.

COMMENT: In his talk with Buck, the supervisor was more direct and commanding than the supervisors in the other two cases. All of these examples involved violations of company policies, but Buck's case also had legal implications and was a second offense. He had been accused of sexual harassment once before.

The supervisor also found that leading questions didn't draw out useful ideas from Buck for resolving the issue. Buck initially didn't think his remarks were offensive to June. He interpreted her comments to knock it off as a come-on. The points made at the meeting on harassment had gone over his head. The supervisor had to provide information Buck was missing and lead him by the hand until he could see for himself that only one solution to the problem was possible. At the same time, he kept asking Buck what his thoughts were and how he interpreted what he was hearing to make sure he would be able to abide by sexual harassment regulations in the future.

SIMPLER CONFRONTATIONS

The three confrontations above each took several minutes. They often don't need to be that long to be effective. Many day-to-day problems can be straightened out quickly by confronting the persons responsible, as in the following case involving two co-workers.

JAN: Tom tells me your requests for material come to him with too short a lead time for him to get it in from the mill before you need it. What do you think you can do about it?

BOB: I'll put him on the route sheet as soon as we get the specifications from engineering. That will give him the most time to place his orders.

JAN: That's fine, Tom. The more time the better, because it gives him more leeway to negotiate freight rates.

BOB: I'll speed it up, Jan.

COMMENT: If you know how to state the issue precisely and let the other person take the lead in how it's to be solved, many situations like this can be handled on the spot. **Don't hesitate to lay problems before your workers.** They know a lot about what's going on in their areas and can often provide some good solutions. What's more, if the solution is theirs, you can be pretty sure they'll do all they can to make it work.

EXERCISE #1

Now that you've seen some examples of how constructive confronting works, it's time to try it out. Can you think of some problem in your own unit that might be solved by constructive confronting? It might be a worker who gets into arguments that disrupt schedules, or failure to put away tools at the end of a shift and leave a neat workplace, or too long coffee breaks.

As you did in Chapter 9, write out on the lines below or on a sheet of paper an opening statement that defines the issue clearly and concisely.

_____

_____

_____

_____

_____

Now try to imagine a few different replies the person you're confronting might make.

_____

_____

_____

_____

What would your next question or statement be to keep the discussion on track and moving toward the solution of the issue?

_____

_____

_____

_____

_____

What would you say to bring the issue to a head and put
the responsibility on the other person to come up with a
solution?

_____

_____

_____

_____

_____

EXERCISE #2

Having thought about the problem and how you would
deal with it, watch for the next time the issue comes up at
work and give constructive confronting a try. Even if it
doesn't go smoother, you'll learn from the experience.
While the interview is still fresh in your mind, write it
down -- what you said, what the other person said. Then
analyze it in the light of this and preceding chapters to see
what you did right and where you need to improve.

14

ENDING CONFRONTATION
ON A POSITIVE NOTE

The dialogues in the last chapter can be analyzed to show the rise and fall of emotions as the confrontation progressed.

The opening statement of the issue presented the confrontee with a challenge that sometimes evoked a hostile response. Unless the problem could be readily and simply solved, tempers might rise, despite the confronter's effort to keep the discussion objective and impersonal. By persistently bringing the question back to the central issue, the confronter gradually nudged the person confronted into a more adult state of mind where the issue could be resolved. Emotion and resentment toward the confronter subsided, and the confronter took advantage of the better atmosphere to pull the sting out of the confrontation with some complimentary remark.

The closing is another place where you capitalize on the "constructive" in confronting. Remember that this book is about empowerment as well as supervision. By confronting your workers, you are empowering them to think for themselves and reach their own decisions. You are releasing them from the old bondage of "Do as I say and don't ask why." The closing of the confrontation gives you an opportunity to drive home this point.

The signoff might be simply "okay, that's behind us." or "Let's get back to work. We've settled that," but **both** parties should leave feeling good about themselves, because together they had accomplished something in putting a troublesome issue to rest.

A positive ending to a confrontation is certainly less difficult than the problem solving stage, or even stating the issue. It calls for no special skills. Closing remarks to compensate for any resentment that might have built up during the confrontation have only one critical test: they must be genuine and sincere.

This is one place where your past interaction with your workers pays off. If you know your workers and pay daily attention to them, a word of praise from you now means a lot to them. But if you've been distant and aloof, a compliment such as "You're one of our best workers" will sound hollow and self-serving. The worker may say, "Thanks," but be thinking, "What does he know about me or what I do?"

If the worker has been cooperative in the problem solving stage, or has come around to a reasonable position from initial antagonism, you can always express appreciation for the way in which the worker thought through the issue. The process is important in itself, because it is a means for developing the ability to think logically. **It is the essence of empowerment.** Logical thinking is evidence that a person is an adult who has "put away childish things," as the Bible says. That's worth a compliment.

It's best to keep the closing fairly brief. Don't drag it out or let your complimentary remarks become overblown. By saying too much, you'll make yourself less believable. Although you may enjoy a generally good relationship with the person you confronted and have things you could talk about, now is not the time for it. Don't let the confrontation tail off into irrelevancies. It's a serious business, and you want the person to go off thinking about the conclusion you reached and how you reached it, not about the next night's bowling.

As in everything you're learning about supervising

empowered workers, putting a positive ending on a confrontation won't become real to you until you do it in practice. Therefore, the place to acquire the skill is off the job. Exercise #1 below will help prepare you for the real thing.

EXERCISE #1

Go back to the exercise you did at the end of the preceding chapter. If you've had a chance to try out constructive confronting on the job, so much the better.

Think about the situation you identified and the individual in your unit who might be involved. Assume you have gone through the problem solving stage successfully. Now write down a sentence or two you think would be appropriate to end the confrontation on a positive note.

_____

_____

_____

_____

_____

Here are five endings others have found useful:

"We worked our way through that issue pretty well. You're a good thinker."

"Your work stands up real well. Glad we're in the same unit."

"I'm glad to get this behind us. Let's get on with it."

"We've got a basis now to move ahead. Things should work out okay."

"I'm glad we had this talk. It helps to see both sides."

EXERCISE #2

If you have tried constructive confronting on the job, give your estimate of the result and why you think it went the way it did.

_____ very satisfactory. Issue resolved.

_____ partially satisfactory. Some progress.

_____ not very satisfactory. Confrontation bogged down.

_____ a dismal failure.

The main reasons for the result were _____

_____

_____

_____

If you haven't tried on-the-job confronting yet, plan to do so soon and come back to the above with your rating and reasons for its success or failure.

15

WHEN PEOPLE WON'T
PROBLEM SOLVE

The great majority of workers will respond positively to
the supervisor who confronts them constructively. They
will take the lead offered to them and try to come up with
solutions to the problem at hand. However, the system
won't work easily all the time, and there are occasionally
individuals with whom it won't work at all.

In Chapter 13, you saw how difficult it was for the
supervisor to get Buck to face up to the issue of sexual
harassment. The supervisor had to go back and explain a
lot of stuff that most people would take for granted.
Somehow, Buck's outlook and attitudes hadn't changed
with the times, and it took patience on the supervisor's
part before Buck recognized that he was violating company
rules and the law of the land.

Some workers will need more help than others before
they can problem solve. **You may have to fill gaps in
their information or teach them how to reason
logically.** Too bad you have to spend time with them on
basics they should have picked up as children at home or
in school, but there are a great many underprivileged and
deprived people in the workforce. A job is just about their
last chance to catch up on what they've missed.

Those who are unable to reason well may try to conceal
their shortcomings with hostility or indifference. Don't give
up on them. Once you have won their trust through daily
interacting, these defenses will melt away, and you can

begin to use your supervisory skills to bring them up to speed.

ROADBLOCK SIGNS

Angry or rebellious responses to your questions are signs that the person confronted is not about to take on the responsibility of solving a problem. The worker may come forward with such replies as, "That's your problem, not mine," or "Everybody else does it. Why pick on me?"

Another barrier to the process is silence. The worker stonewalls the confrontation, or perhaps makes some evasive reply, such as, "I don't know," or "Why ask me?"

If clarifying the obvious fails to open a path for discussion, you may have to exert the authority of your position, explaining that it's your job to see that things are done right and that you will, if necessary, impose a decision upon the worker.

You might say to the worker, "Look, I'm giving you a chance to help solve this problem in your own way, but if you don't want to do this, I'll have no choice but to decide it my way, whether you like it or not."

If there's a glimmer of hope that the worker's attitude may be changing, you can jump start the stalled discussion by backing up a bit with a question, "Tell me, what do you think the issue is?"

Try not to let your irritation show through. Keep a calm tone of voice and be sincere in your desire to reach a solution that is mutually satisfying. Remember that the worker is probably wrestling inside with all sorts of emotions -- embarrassment, resentment, shame, hurt, pride or fear. Use your skills to ease tension and get the conversation going in an adult, problem solving mode, and some sensible ideas will begin to come out.

WHEN TO CALL A HALT

If resistance persists in spite of your best efforts, you have two choices on what to do next:

1. Stop the confrontation and reschedule it for a later time, after the worker has had a chance to think it over. A second meeting may be more fruitful.

2. Close the confrontation by telling the worker,

    "I would have liked more ideas from you on what to do. But without them, this is how it is going to be."

Then you state your decision and say what you expect of the worker in the future. In a sense, this is a step backward into the old way of telling workers what to do instead of leading them to figure it out for themselves. Don't use it unless it is clear that more talking at this time will do no good.

EVALUATE WHAT HAPPENED

Always evaluate your own handling of a confrontation to see if there might be better ways to do it next time. You are sure to improve with practice, and constructive confronting will become easier as your work group begins to understand the process.

REFERRALS

There are rare instances of workers whose mental and emotional processes are so mixed up or underdeveloped that it is impossible for them to problem solve. Supervisors may now and then encounter habitual disruptive behavior or substandard performance that does not respond to constructive confronting or to any form of discipline, possibly due to some deep-seated mental or emotional problem.

Your supervisory skills can carry you only so far with serious traumas of this sort. As will be discussed in Chapter 18, you can provide helpful personal discussion up to a point. Beyond this, it is important to recognize the need for outside help and know where and when to look for it. Your human resources department or personnel manager should usually be brought in at this point.

SUMMARY

This ends the six-chapter look at the ways and benefits of **constructive confrontation.** You have seen that constructive confronting gets workers to think for themselves. You have probably also sensed that constructive confronting is a "tough and human" form of discipline because it asks workers to take the lead in solving their own job challenges and to do something about their personal shortcomings. As such, it stimulates their self motivation and personal growth. It also sets the stage for **empowering** workers with a say in how they do their jobs, a practice which is described in the next two chapters.

16

WHAT WORKER
EMPOWERMENT MEANS

If the manager above you is letting you do your job, you are empowered to do a number of important things without having to check with your boss. You have a good deal of say about how things are done in your unit.

For example, you can decide who is to be in your work group. If one worker is incompetent or causes a lot of trouble, you can decide what's to be done about it. You can specify tools and equipment for your group. You can assign jobs within your group, make judgments on granting time off and interpret company policies.

Some supervisors are afraid to use all the power they have. They go to their boss for decisions they could make themselves, because they are still following habits formed in an earlier day when they were always told what to do.

Of course, there are areas where you are not free to make decisions. You can't change blueprints, substitute specified materials or depart from tolerances in customer orders. You must adhere to production schedules, packing specifications and the like. But the general rule today is: These are the results you have to achieve. Exercise judgment in how to do it within company policy.

Successful companies in today's competitive markets are pushing power downward and eliminating layers of middle management. They are cutting bureaucracy and excessive reporting requirements. More management responsibility is being laid on first-line supervision. You have been empowered to make more decisions than any generation of supervisors in history.

This power is given to you with the expectation that you in turn will pass much of it along to workers in your group, so that they may become a largely self-directing team. **Your job now is to empower them.** In doing so, you have to decide when to let loose of your authority and how much to give to others. You have to keep some responsibilities -- bigger ones perhaps than you've had before, but fewer of them. You can download a lot of the work you always thought you had to do yourself.

If you doubt that your workers can handle more responsibility for the way they do their jobs, think of all the bosses you have had. Can you remember one who would never let you do things in your own way or at your own pace, who was always on your back to make sure you did it her way? How did that make you feel? You probably thought, "What does she take me for? Does she think I'm all that dumb and can't be trusted?"

If you're still bossing in an old-fashioned way, maybe your workers have the same thoughts about you. It's time then to change. People have more ability than they get credit for. Being constantly told what to do gets them down. They get to feeling that they have no control whatever over what happens at work. **Recognition that a person has some common sense and is capable of doing a job is the foundation of worker empowerment.** Its denial is a putdown that destroys worker initiative and morale.

Empowering your workers gives them a chance to exercise their minds and develop their skills. It makes them feel good about themselves and answers their basic human need for recognition as individuals with worth. In return, they will work smarter and harder, with less fatigue. Productivity has increased dramatically in many companies where worker empowerment has become a way of life. Employer and employee benefit alike.

FIVE COMMON MISTAKES

Some supervisors who admit that worker empowerment sounds good still balk at it. It's hard for them to let loose of their hard-won authority. The old way of just telling people what to do seemed a lot easier than expecting them to make some decisions. Consequently, some supervisors who try to change their styles slip back into the ways they are used to. Here are five common mistaken beliefs that often block supervisors from seeing the benefits of worker empowerment:

1. It's Not the Way We Do Things Around Here.

True. But in the past, business was growing so fast you could get by with inefficiency. Productivity of each worker could be less than 100% and the company could still compete. It's different today. You need the best from every employee to make it in the world market. This means the old ways aren't good enough.

2. I don't want to give my power away. It gives me status and clout.

That's natural. You worked your way up and paid your dues under a boss who told you what to do and made you toe the mark. Now it's your turn. Why give your power away? Two reasons.

First, you'll get turned-on instead of turned-off performance from your workers, and this will lead your unit to become more productive.

Second, your job will become easier. You won't have to stay on top of your workers to make them perform. Develop your standards, and they will find ways to meet them. Your power actually grows when you share it, because your subordinates appreciate having a say in how they do their work and support and respect you as their leader. Being the highly regarded head of a productive unit gives you superior status in the organization.

3. I feel I can make decisions better than my workers.

Maybe so, but how can your workers ever learn to make good decisions unless you give them a chance? One woman supervisor in a creative department tells this story.

"We have to satisfy some persnickity customers. When their orders came in, I used to think I was the only one who could make decisions on how to handle them. I did their work myself or told my staff exactly how to do it. The staff resented it, because it kept them from getting experience they needed and recognition they deserved. My boss took me to task and told me to start passing these tough jobs on to the staff. Since then, I've been more of a delegator, letting the staff do the work and make decisions. This has put new life in our department, and we're doing a better job overall. Admitting that the staff could do as well or better than I could was a bitter pill to swallow, but it cured me of the idea that I had to do everything."

4. I'm not sure I know how to empower my workers.

New things are perplexing, but worker empowerment is easier to learn than you might think. It calls for a change in attitude on your part, rather than a lot of new techniques. If you're willing to ask a worker how he or she thinks something might be done better, or to assign responsibility to a small team, that may be all it takes. The assignment might be to assemble a product, run a service desk, refurbish returned goods and get them back on the shelf, put out a printed monthly flyer, or any other function or project.

Workers have a way of organizing themselves and coming through when given the opportunity. A large western telephone company tried a test with 126 of their customer service teams. **Half of the teams** were allowed to manage themselves, setting their own work schedules, deciding who does what, answering customer inquiries without day-to-day supervision and resolving differences that come up among themselves. **The other half** continued under traditional supervision as usual. The self-managing teams out-performed the directed teams in productivity, cost containment, customer satisfaction, quality of work and safety. Members of the self-managing teams also expressed greater satisfaction with their personal growth and social relationships and had more trust and confidence in the telephone company's management than did the traditionally-supervised teams.

5. **I'm afraid if I do empower my workers, I won't be able to handle them.**

Yes, this is a fear among many veteran supervisors, but you won't be trying something new unprepared. When you have learned the skills of positive interacting and constructive confronting, you are equipped to lead your empowered workers. Through interacting with them, you recognize your workers as important to the organization, and they are in a frame of mind to want to act responsibly. When given a say in how they do their jobs, they are then in a mood to do their best. If they make some faulty judgments from time to time, your confronting skills enable them to think through how to get back on track.

Worker empowerment means giving workers power to make some decisions in matters affecting their jobs. Whether they receive this power depends on you, their supervisor. You have the power to empower them.

EXERCISE #1

Write down three or four areas of your current supervison you think you might be able to hand over to members of your unit.

_____

_____

_____

_____

_____

EXERCISE #2

List areas you think you can't transfer to anyone else.

_____

_____

_____

_____

_____

17

LEADING SELF-MANAGING TEAMS

The nature of the work determines the degree of worker involvement in decision making. We call these degrees **suggestion involvement, job involvement and high involvement.**

SUGGESTION INVOLVEMENT

On simple, repetitive jobs, there are not a great many decisions to be made on **how** the work is to be done. Once procedures are established, the chances to vary from them are limited. However, there are other opportunities for worker input. These are some of the areas where workers can have an input;

Hand tool features	Lighting
Work table layout	Utility of bench or chair
Choice of fasteners	Overtime practices
Design of jigs, fixtures	Washroom accessories
Materials handling	Canteen options
Storage systems	After hours activities
Car parking	Security provisions
Bulletin boards	Employee communications
Suggestion systems	Grievances procedures
Noise abatement	Safety measures

Employee involvement at this level gives workers an opportunity to make suggestions. Although they don't have the authority to make changes on their own, just being heard makes them feel that their ideas have value and will have a bearing on decisions that affect them. Asking employees for suggestions defuses grumbling, gets gripes out into the open and can bring forth workable ideas that have real merit.

Suggestion boxes are designed for this purpose, but they yield a less satisfactory response than personal contact between the supervisor and the members of the unit. By involving yourself in the process, you make a statement that you and the company really care about what your workers think and how they feel. No impersonal system can convey these sentiments, nor can formal programs such as quality circles take the place of daily informal interaction between supervisor and employee.

Suggestion involvement is especially applicable in such automated operations as stamping, machine tending, medical lab testing, order entry or telephone switching, where technology leaves little room for variation from routine. However, there are many non-routine areas of the job that are open to change.

What You Need to Do

As a supervisor in this kind of work situation, you should find time to talk with employees and encourage them to volunteer ideas for improvement. Let your people know their thoughts are welcome. Be attentive to suggestions and look for good in them before seeking reasons why they won't work. Be alert for other ways an idea might be applied. Even if it's way off base, thank the worker for suggesting it and encourage another try. If the worker disagrees with your explanation of why an idea is unworkable, use your constructive confronting skills to explore the differences between your two views, and always leave the discussion on a positive note.

If the idea is workable, give the worker full credit and make sure the rest of the unit knows about it. If it's significant enough, try to get it written up in the company publication and recommend the employee for a cash award, if your company has an award program.

JOB INVOLVEMENT

One step up from being open to suggestions is to grant individuals and teams a say in how they do their jobs. You give them authority to build components or products within general specifications, or to provide services or process information, or to make schedules or approve new hires, subject to general policy guidelines. This level of involvement is true decision sharing.

With today's technology, skilled workers with special training are in demand. They have to share complex information with each other and make many joint decisions. People with various kinds of know-how have to work together, often crossing old departmental lines. Those capable of working with new technologies are smart enough to direct their own efforts to a large extent and to function effectively in a team. As a supervisor, you don't have to tell them what to do and how to do it. You can empower them to make a lot of job decisions themselves.

Take, for example, physical therapists working in a hospital. They are technically trained and highly specialized employees who must work with physicians, nurses and other technicians in providing total patient care. Cases involving disabilities or dysfunctions, such as loss of knee flexion, are assigned to a therapist for rehabilitation. The therapist analyzes the problem and decides what type of therapy the patient needs. The physician approves and monitors the treatment. The nurse back in the ward observes improvement and reports on the patient's progress to the physician and the therapist. With the physician's concurrence, the therapist decides when treatment should be discontinued.

What you have here is a self-managing team. The supervisor of the physical therapy department has managerial responsibilities, but telling the therapist **what** to do is not one of them.

HIGH INVOLVEMENT

This goes even further than giving employees a say in how they do their jobs. It lets them organize and run their own work. Salespersons on the road and repair technicians have generally been granted high involvement status, mainly because they are away from the office and close supervision over them is not practical.

However, workers in production, service or administration can also become largely self-managing, if the supervisor has the skill and the desire to let it happen and prepares the workers to accept the responsibility.

Four Steps to Remember

The supervisor who wants to raise the involvement level of a work unit needs to take four steps:

1. Talk over standards of performance and behavior with the group until there is agreement on what is acceptable.

2. As workers prove they are able to handle freedom, give them more of it. Grant independence a step at a time. Have subordinates write-out what activities and performance results they want to be accountable for.

3. Have workers measure the degree to which standards have been met or surpassed.

4. Confront deficiencies in a constructive way and praise achievement. Reward superior performance with raises or bonuses to the extent company policy permits.

You'll find most workers can be trained to manage themselves if standards and measures of accountability are in place.

EXERCISE

1. Think about the unit you supervise. To what degree are your subordinates involved in decisions of the workplace?

   _____ Can make suggestions but not decisions.

   _____ Can make some job-related decisions.

   _____ Can make most decisions affecting the job.

   _____ Highly involved. Largely self- managing.

2. Would you like to increase your unit's involvement?

   _____ Yes _____ No _____ Not sure

3. What do you think you would have to learn to:

   a. Get your workers to make suggestions.

   _____

   _____

   _____

   _____

   _____

   b. Give your workers a say in how they do their jobs.

   _____

   _____

   _____

   _____

   _____

c. Make your unit largely self-managing.

_____

_____

_____

_____

_____

This ends the two chapters on empowering workers and leading self-managing teams. Now, to other kinds of employee encounters.

18

COUNSELING AND NEGOTIATING

The Big Three people skills you have learned -- how to talk to your people, getting them to solve their own problems and sharing your decision-making authority with them -- will be useful in two other areas that are somewhat related to constructive confronting, but that differ from it in purpose and technique. These areas are **counseling** and **negotiating.** Let's review.

In **constructive confronting,** you are trying to get a person to think through a problem and figure out a solution. You encourage a worker to take the lead in resolving the issue. You impose a solution only as a last resort after it becomes clear that the worker is either unable or unwilling to come up with a valid answer. You involve the worker as much as you can, but when the worker won't, or can't, problem solve, you reach a solution for them. The purpose of confronting is twofold:

1. To solve the problem.

2. To develop reasoning capacity and self reliance in the worker.

Counseling a subordinate with a personal, off-the-job problem doesn't involve the company directly. You encourage the subordinate to find a solution, as in confronting, but you never impose a solution, because your authority does not extend to the worker's personal life. You help by listening, clarifying the worker's thoughts, filling in gaps in information, and pointing out resources that are available.

If the problem proves to be too much for the subordinate to solve alone, you encourage their turning to professional help, especially if company policies provide for such services.

In **negotiating** on-the-job issues with subordinates, **you** take the initiative to find a settlement. The purpose of negotiating is to reach agreement on the terms of the settlement. You don't dictate the terms, nor do you put the burden of resolving the issue on the other party. You, as supervisor, **do take an active role** in seeking a solution that will be beneficial to your interests.

Each side is responsible for presenting its views and for trading off point-against-point until the conditions are arranged in a way that both parties can accept. You win some points and lose others, but if the main core of what you want comes through intact, you're a winner overall. And there does not have to be a loser. Both sides may get most of what they want.

These are the distinctions and similarities in three of the major tools supervisors use. We have covered confronting. Now let's take a more detailed look at how you can practice personal counseling and negotiating.

COUNSELING SUBORDINATES

When your people come to you, their boss, with personal problems, take it as a compliment. It means they trust you and respect your judgment. But neither you nor they should expect that you can take all their troubles away. What you can do is help them see their problems clearly and possibly find their own solutions. Or, you may be able to point them in directions where they can find more specific help. Problems you might hear about include:

Marital difficulties	Sending children to college
Mortgage or car payments	Drug addiction
Health crises	Need for more education
Alcoholism	

There are many other problems that on the surface have nothing to do with work. Yet they can be distractions from work and a drag on performance and productivity. This is reason enough for you and the company to be concerned, apart from the concern that all people of good will should have toward each other.

You are not a trained social worker, psychologist or clergyman, and you shouldn't try to assume their roles, but you are qualified to help your subordinates within limits by following this clear and straightforward process:

1. Listen to the worker's account of the problem.

2. Draw out essential facts that seem to be missing in the worker's statement of the case.

3. Ask the worker, "Have you thought of any ways your problem might be solved?"

4. If the answer is "yes," ask what they are.

5. If the answer is "no," ask, "Can you think of any ways now?"

6. Go over the various ways considered and ask what the worker thinks the consequences of each solution might be.

7. Encourage the worker to select what seems to be **their** best solution and to plan and follow through on their course of action to correct the problem.

Note that throughout the process, **you refrain** from giving advice on how your subordinate ought to solve the problem. You act as a sounding board for the person's own ideas, leaving the solution up to the worker. You can't require the worker to find a solution or have one imposed, because you don't have that authority in this situation.

Besides clarifying the problem and helping the worker to develop solutions and pick the best among them, you can **provide information** that may be needed to plan and carry out the solution. For example, you can interpret company policies that may be applicable and explain available company benefits and services or community resources that may be called upon. This helps the worker deal with the facts and start taking positive action.

At no point should you grab the ball. Holding off from giving advice, even when it's requested, is not a cop out. Many of the best professional counselors follow the same practice. They've found that normal people can solve their own problems, if they know the facts and keep a clear head to develop enough alternatives for a choice of actions to take. Also, by restraining yourself from proposing a solution, you can't be blamed if it doesn't work out.

Personal problems may take more than one discussion before they can be resolved. Don't rush it. Set a time to meet again and give your worker a chance to think over what has been said.

Don't expect 100% success in your counseling. Not everyone is what we call "normal." Some people can't think things through without more professional help than you are equipped to give. If several meetings haven't produced a satisfactory result, your responsibility is to refer the worker through your human resources department to someone professionally trained in dealing with underlying personality problems. You are a valuable first-aid station, but don't try to be the doctor.

Resisting the impulse to give advice when asked is the biggest challenge facing most supervisors in off-the-job personal counseling. Observe how the supervisor avoids this pitfall in the following example.

THE SITUATION: The employee was taking a computer course at company expense in the hope of qualifying for a better job. The supervisor noted that he seemed depressed and that his work was falling below his usual standards. He decided to try to find out what was wrong.

SUPV: You haven't been yourself lately. Is something hanging over you?

EMPL: Yeah, there sure is.

SUPV: Want to tell me about it? We have some time now.

EMPL: OK. I'm sort of embarrassed about it. See, I'm taking this computer course in night school and the company's paying the tuition. Fact is, I'm getting failing grades and may flunk out unless I get more time to study.

SUPV: What's standing in your way?

EMPL: Well, my daughter is staying with us until she has her baby, and that sort of cramps us and makes it hard to concentrate. Then I've been adding a room onto the house and that takes a lot of my spare time.

SUPV: Anything else?

EMPL: On top of that, I'm in this exercise program and am supposed to run every day. So I don't have much time to read the computer book. Class night just comes around too soon.

SUPV: So you know all the things that are standing in your way. Now how do you size up the situation?

EMPL: Gosh, I don't know. My wife keeps nagging at me to get that room finished. I lose sleep worrying and I'm not doing too well on the job. I seem to be going around in circles. What do you think I should do?

SUPV: Is that the way you size up the situation?

EMPL: It's a poor way to deal with it, I know, but I really don't have any handle on it. What would you advise me to do?

SUPV: How might you go about sizing it up?

EMPL: I'm not sure. Lay out each problem in order, I guess. See how they fit together. What do you think?

SUPV: What kind of order?

EMPL: Well, to take my daughter first. Her husband is overseas. We have to see her through this. The baby is due in about three weeks. After that, she's going to move in with his parents, so that will take care of that.

SUPV: OK. That's one down.

EMPL: As far as the house is concerned, I could take my time with that. No great sweat.

SUPV: Well, that's two down.

EMPL: My wife nags at me most of the time anyway, so I guess I can grin and bear it for awhile.

SUPV: So now, what's left?

EMPL: It wouldn't kill me to cut down on the exercise, but that leaves me still so far behind on the computer course, I'd have to play fast catch up to pull through. The company expects me to complete it, and I want to. But what am I going to do? I can't quit my job to study all the time.

SUPV: Did you know that Janet, my secretary, took that course last year and was a whiz at it? Janet's the type who would be glad to help you get up to speed, I think.

EMPL: Sure, I remember. She did take that course. She could be my savior. I think I'll ask her. I'd sure like to get over this hump. It's bugging the sap out of me.

SUPV: Sounds like you've got a handle on it now.

EMPL: I think I do. I'll delay the room, cut the exercise, and sweat out the next three weeks one way or another to make room for our daughter. If Janet will give me a hand, I can still pass that course. It sure helps to talk things over with you. I appreciate your time. I shouldn't really bother you with such problems, but your advice has been a big help.

SUPV: Let's keep in touch. You have a good head on your shoulders and you used it to figure this one out. Don't hesitate to come to me any time something like this comes up and you want to talk.

EMPL: Thanks a lot. See you.

In this dialogue, note how the supervisor provided the framework for the worker to think through, sort out, deal with and move ahead on the wrenching problem that only a few minutes before had the worker's mind tied up in knots. Although the worker's impression was that he had received advice, the supervisor actually gave none. Through a series of short questions, the worker was guided toward an orderly examination of the facts and encouraged to develop solutions on his own. The supervisor added the new knowledge that Janet might be available as a resource, and this was incorporated in the worker's course of action.

The solution to the problem might appear to have come too quickly and easily, but this is exactly what happens in most personal counseling situations. The reason for this is that people with problems usually have in the back of their heads several possible solutions. They may be confused as to which course to take, or worried about the consequences. It may take no more than a few pointed questions to get them off dead center. The process is not one of creating solutions, but rather of drawing out those that are probably already there.

HOW TO NEGOTIATE

You're probably familiar with the way labor-management negotiations proceed. The union wants such things as higher wages, improved benefits, or changes in work rules for its members. The company says it can't afford to meet union demands and may counter by seeking concessions from the union. The two sides are far apart, so they sit down to the table to negotiate. Negotiators work toward agreement.

Negotiation at the individual level, while not in the public eye, is going on every day on the used car lot, in the family living room where TV watching vs. homework is an issue, and in many other areas of life, including the workplace. As a supervisor, you should think of negotiation as a far more effective tool than the old blunt instruments of one-sided decisions. Here are some examples of situations where negotiation is the supervisor's tool of choice.

YOUR SIDE

You want a worker to switch days off.

You want someone to work overtime on a weekend to

to get an order out.

You're introducing a procedure a worker doesn't like.

WORKER'S SIDE

Wants to switch days off with another employee.

Asks for transfer to another machine.

Wants time off when work schedule is especially heavy.

In seeking solutions that are beneficial to your side, yet agreeable to the other party, be sure to **separate your emotions from the facts of the issue.** Your emotions might be anger, blame, defensiveness, pride, envy, pity, or generosity. These are all natural feelings, but they can lessen your ability to think and act clearly in give-and-take negotiations. To be an effective negotiator, you need to disengage your emotions from your thinking and deal with the merits of the problem.

Focus on the interests each party really wants to protect, not on stated positions. Avoid starting negotiations from a fixed position -- the other party's or your own. Think about what the real interests are that each of you wants to preserve and start with an open mind as to how they will be preserved. Examine the facts surrounding the issue and rank them in terms of their importance to each party in reaching an agreement. The final agreement should square with the facts and satisfy the primary interests of both parties. For a settlement to stand up, both sides have to feel that it was the best one available.

Generate a variety of options for solving the issue. The first few ideas presented by either side are unlikely to provide enough choices for a mutually acceptable solution. Keep searching for more alternatives, perhaps eight or ten. Some may not be the answer, but will trigger better ideas. Spend more time in developing alternatives than in trying to choose which alternative is best, because you'll probably wind up combining the best parts of several.

Insist on using objective criteria for selecting the best solution. You need some generally accepted standard to measure whether your final solution is fair to all. Such standards might be the going wage rate from a recent survey, expert opinion, recognized medical procedures, the union contract, the company personnel handbook, preventive maintenance schedules, time standards, or manuals specifying machine ratings, capacities and repair requirements.

These guidelines for negotiation are impartial and should be acceptable to both sides. They establish a level playing field where issues can be settled on the basis of merit rather than management authority or employee ultimatum. To reach a settlement, there are seven key rules you should follow:

1. **Have goals that are fair and supportable.**

2. **Take the initiative in presenting your requirements.**

3. **Relate your bargaining to the other person's needs.**

4. **Look for common grounds.**

5. **Give ground grudgingly. Get concessions in exchange for giving concessions.**

6. **Separate the issues.**

7. **Reach a fair agreement.**

In the following dialogue between a supervisor and a worker, note how the supervisor follows these points.

ED: I've got to be making more money! I turn out the best units in the department, and I'm worth more to the company than the rest of those jokers.

SUPV: Can't do it, Ed. I know you're the best in the department, but you're already at the top of the wage range. Until the range is raised, you can't go any higher.

ED: Baloney! There are ways for you to break the ceiling. I want you to do it. If you don't, I'm going to have to look for another place to work. I'm in a money bind.

SUPV: Well, I can't take you beyond the range. But I can schedule you on some field installation work. Those trips carry thirty percent premium pay plus travel expenses and a flat amount for living expense.

ED: You know I can't do that. My wife works a full shift, too. I can't be gone on those three and four day installations.

SUPV: We just took on a new product that requires only one and two day trips. What if I assigned you to some of those?

ED: That'd be fine if I didn't have to go more than two or three trips a month.

SUPV: I think we can handle that, Ed. Whatta you say we try it?

ED: Sounds like a good deal to me. Let's do it. But

give me a week to clear things at home. My wife and I will have to arrange the kid's schedules.

SUPV: That's okay, Ed. You're on.

The supervisor in this case protected the company goal of not exceeding the wage rate. He found common ground for negotiation -- getting more money for Ed. He used the wage range as an objective standard against which to hold his ground. He took the initiative in coming up with extra money through field installation work. He gave ground by agreeing to assign Ed to no more than three trips per month, and got a concession from Ed that he would begin traveling within one week. Overall, the supervisor negotiated Ed's need for more money without exceeding the wage rate and retained Ed's good will as a valuable producer.

Ed also gained from the negotiation by getting more money, his real concern, and by finding a field assignment that fitted into his home schedule.

From this example, you can see how negotiations differ from confronting and counseling. In **confronting,** the supervisor tries to get the subordinate to take the lead in finding a solution to the problem, imposing one only if the subordinate won't or can't problem-solve. In **counseling** a subordinate with a personal problem, the supervisor is a listener, encouraging the subordinate to figure out a solution without giving advice, and suggesting outside help if it's needed. In **negotiating,** the supervisor takes the initiative and resolves the issue on the best terms that are fair to both parties.

NOTE: For more information on negotiating, see "Getting to Yes" by Fisher and Ury, which is available in most libraries or bookstores.

19

SKILLS TO HELP YOU COMMUNICATE

How you listen, how you talk and how you look all influence what other people think of you and how they respond to you. The preceding chapters have shown the importance of the words you use and the tone of voice in which you say them. This chapter will give you some **non-verbal** ways to reinforce what you say and help you create the impression you want to make, as well as some additional aids to effective speaking.

To be successful, a supervisor can't be a shrinking violet, but must be self-assertive. Some companies have focused on assertiveness training for their supervisors. Our techniques will help you assert yourself in the right way at the right times without becoming obnoxious.

NON-VERBAL SIGNALS

Let's take these in order, beginning with the impression your appearance makes before you say anything.

1. Dress. The clothes you wear and your personal grooming tell others what you think of them and what you think of yourself. You don't wear blue jeans to a wedding. You dress to fit the occasion. To show up looking anything but your best is an insult to the bride and groom and makes other guests wonder what's wrong with you.

On the other hand, don't over-dress. You've heard people say, "She looks like a Christmas tree."

There's an appropriate style of dress for every time and place, including the workplace. Coat and tie may be right for the office but wrong in the shop. If your job as supervisor calls for protective clothing or a white coat, keep it as neat as you can. Be careful of personal hygiene so that breath or body odor don't offend, and see that hair is well groomed.

Your appearance is your opening statement. First impressions sometimes stick.

2. Entrances. The way you walk in also makes a statement. If you shuffle in like an absent-minded professor, your workers will wonder whether you're at all aware of them and on top of your job. Hesitant, timid entrances convey uncertainty and lack of authority.

A decisive entrance with upright posture signals confidence and purpose.

3. Handshake. Don't be a jellyfish or a bone crusher when you shake hands. A weak, flabby handshake suggests uncertainty and inferiority. Excessive pressure suggests an overbearing aggressiveness and bullying nature. Offer a firm and confident grip that doesn't inflict pain, and you establish a basis where you and the other person can talk reasonably.

If you run into some bear whose handshake makes **you** wince, push your hand as far inside his as you can to reduce his leverage. This will make it hard for the big brute to hurt you, and it will also give you a firmer handshake.

4. Eye contact. You no doubt mistrust shifty-eyed people and tend to shrink from those who stare or "look a hole through you." How do others feel about the way you look at them? Your eyes express much about what you think, feel and intend. When you make eye-to-eye contact with someone, you signal that they have your interest and attention.

Eye contact that is relaxed, natural and comfortable opens a path of communication. Give your eyes some real work to do in exploring the other person's thoughts and feelings through their eyes, rather than looking inward on your own anxieties, suspicions or embarrassments. The contact need not be continuous or always direct. At a distance of four feet or so, any focus within a six inch radius of the other person's eyes will appear as eye contact. Relieve the intensity from time to time by looking away briefly at other points of interest.

5. Facial expression. Your face naturally expresses your thoughts and feelings. Don't try to mask them. It will only make you uncomfortable and the other person mistrustful. Let your face play its part in conveying the message you want to send, whether it's a compliment or a criticism, pleasure or displeasure.

6. Body space. In some countries, faces will be within a few inches of each other when two people are talking. In the United States, we like to keep more distance and feel uncomfortable when someone gets too close.

We have other conventions in space relationships. Height gives the impression of superiority. The judge's bench is above the rest of the courtroom. Humphrey Bogart stood on a box for closeups with taller leading ladies. George Raft wore elevator shoes.

In conversation, someone who is standing up has an advantage over one who is seated in a chair. Sitting behind a desk says to the person opposite, "I'm important." At banquets, being at the speaker's table carries distinction.

Supervisors should use these behavior conditioners thoughtfully to send the right messages. The rule of thumb is to extend equality to others for the sake of good communication.

7. Body posture. Body movements also send unspoken messages. When standing to speak before a group, arms should be relaxed at the sides until a meaningful gesture to emphasize words is called for. Otherwise, natural head movements are sufficient to hold attention. Twisting hands, straightening the tie, head scratching or leaning on the desk or podium are only distractions. While sitting, a relaxed upright position with feet on the floor or crossed at the ankles makes a confident, poised statement. Slouching, crossing the legs, or throwing an arm across the back of the chair makes a casual, informal statement, which is occasionally what you want to put someone at ease, but use it sparingly.

8. Voice characteristics. Chapter twelve, "Tone of Voice Tells the Truth," discusses in detail the difference between "how" something is said and "what" is said. The quality of voice should agree with the nature of the message. Business conversations are best conducted at moderate volume, with pitch in the lower rather than the higher ranges. They should have enough variation in pace to hold interest and add clarity.

9. Listening. Being a good listener is just as important as being a good talker. Listening is an active process, not a passive one. You can choose how carefully you want to listen to someone talking, depending on your judgment of the importance of the subject, after you've heard enough to identify it.

Polite listening is the lowest level. You hear enough to get the general gist and make a reply. Then your mind moves on to something else. Remarks about the weather, the ball game and other small talk fall in this category. The other person doesn't expect you to carry on beyond an acknowledgment and perhaps a few words to close.

The **attentive** level is reserved for information that has some significance. You listen carefully enough to salt it away in your memory bank, repeating it if necessary to be sure you've got it right. A report on the status of a job, the date of a delivery, or other factual matter fall into this level.

At the **analytical** level, you listen and think deeply about what is being said. Word that a machine has broken down, a request for a change in schedule, a complaint about a co-worker, or good news about a new order are examples of communication that require probing. As you listen, you check your own mind to sense the meaning of what you are hearing and formulate questions to steer and develop a dialogue. Your objective is to fill in the missing parts of a picture.

Knowing how to listen and at what level is one mark of a good supervisor. You don't have to give your full, undivided and prolonged attention to everything.

10. Touching. French and Italian people greet each other with an embrace and kiss without reservation. We're more restrained in this country, but still, many psychologists today are advocating hugging as a sign of caring. Such open demonstrations aren't yet acceptable in most work situations, but moderate physical contact, such as a pat on the back, clasping the forearm during a hand shake, or a touch on arm or shoulder, when appropriate, can improve social relationships and enhance self-respect.

Some individuals feel uncomfortable when they are touched, as if their privacy had been invaded. Their feelings must be respected, but most workers will appreciate the human touch. Use touching selectively.

11. Timing. Jay Leno knows exactly when to time his punch lines to get a laugh. You also have to understand and practice good timing with your workers and with your boss. Picking the right time to introduce a change in procedures has a lot to do with how well it is received. Knowing when to encourage a discussion and when to stop it, when to break into a conversation and when to stay out, when to make a joke and when to be serious -- all are important in asserting your leadership.

A sense of timing is partly a matter of instinct, but it can also be developed through practice. Test yourself on timing and make note of your successes and failures. There is no training ground to compare with your own job.

12. Openness. Your workers deserve to know your true feelings. Otherwise, they never know where they really stand. They can't be sure of what you want or don't want. You do them no favor by being less than open and forthright with them. They will respond to insincerity with concealments of their own, or they will clam up on you.

Expressing how you actually feel requires a measure of self-assertion. It sometimes takes courage, but almost anything can be expressed with confidence if it is stated appropriately and at the right time.

VERBAL SIGNALS

Here are a dozen supplementary techniques to add to the verbal skills you learned in the chapters on interacting and confronting.

1. Keeping conversations going. You've been in discussions that died a painful death, before useful ideas they might have produced had a chance to come out. It needn't be that way. Conversations that flow feed on themselves, one thing leading to another. As a group leader, you can keep conversations alive until you want them to end with the aid of these six prompts.

a. Ask open-ended questions. Any question that can be answered "yes" or "no" is a closed-end question. Instead, ask questions that begin with "How" or "Why" to draw out opinions.

b. Capitalize on free information. People often volunteer a lot of information about themselves. For example, in answer to a question, "How long have you lived here?" the answer might be, "For five years. Since I left

Westinghouse." You can pick up on Westinghouse or what the person did there, good and bad things about the company, etc. Tidbits dropped as free information often lead to the most interesting part of a conversation and to the most valuable ideas..

c. Build self-respect in others. People who respect themselves will open up and not be afraid to come forward with ideas. Those who feel put down will shut up. Acknowledge and applaud every contribution. Avoid and discourage "good-natured ribbing," which is frequently taken amiss.

d. Show interest in others. Good conversationalists ask questions that draw out what another person knows. People like to talk about themselves and the things they're good at. Let them, and see what comes out.

e. Use rituals and ice breakers. In the early stages of a two-way conversation or a group discussion, social formalities help break the ice. "I saw your name on the roster" and "May I get you a cup of coffee?" are typical openers.

A little shop talk or a casual inquiry about family may lead to the discovery of an interest in automobiles, baseball, or barbecue cooking on which to build the conversation and the relationship.

f. Closing out conversation. You call the tune when it's time to quit. Do it in a way that leaves the self-respect of others intact. For example:

I've enjoyed talking with you.

It's been a good discussion. Let's do it again.

I have to leave, but I'll remember what you said.

2. Expressing disagreement. Your workers often disagree with each other, and they may disagree with you.

You may disagree with other supervisors. Honest differences arise on what's best for the work group or the company, and you need a way to settle them calmly, naturally and openly without treading on anyone's self-respect.

As a supervisor, you have to be in command of both the facts and yourself. Whether you are a party to the disagreement or the moderator between two workers, you state up front what the difference is and marshal the evidence. You draw out the conflicting views and then give your conclusion and suggested course of action, qualifying the differences to bring the two sides closer together. You assert yourself, but try not to dictate the solution.

There are times, of course, when two workers can't get together that you will have to decide and say, "Okay. This is the way it's going to be."

3. Asserting yourself in arguments. You can handle arguments on how to run the business by using three approaches:

a. Selective ignoring. When your opponent mixes unfair and abusive statements with fair and objective statements, limit your replies to those that are fair and objective and ignore the rest. This serves to extinguish unfair accusations.

b. The broken record. When you are on firm ground but are still being badgered by side issues and alternate proposals, keep repeating the main point over and over to bring discussion back on track. The "broken record" is a useful rebuttal tool.

c. Sorting out issues. When several issues get intertwined, you aren't going to progress toward a solution until you sort them out and take up each one on its own merits. Sorting requires the ability to analyze and define each issue and the patience to keep the distinctions among them during a heated discussion. If you're ever going to reach a settlement, all parties have to be clear as to the subject on the table.

d. Persuasion. Influencing others to go along with you requires self-assertive skills. Paying attention to the following five points will help your batting average.

1) Try to get on good terms with the people you have to persuade. Sell yourself before you try to sell your idea.

2) Research the other person's needs and situation. The more you know, the better chance you'll have of prevailing.

3) Have something of real value to offer the other person and promote it.

4) Cast your appeal in terms of the other person's interest. Answer their question, "What's in it for me?" before it's asked.

5) Don't hesitate to use "I." Persuasion hinges on open and honest expression. Take responsibility for what you say. "I feel there are a lot of things we can do to help your operation" is more persuasive than "You aren't using our services often enough." The first statement invites a response, "What are they?" The second puts the other person on the defensive and is likely to draw, "We've used your services quite a lot."

4. Protecting yourself from angry attack. When someone attacks you with an angry outburst, your natural reaction is to meet violence with violence. This only escalates the emotion. You have a chance to cool things off by meeting violence with composure. You buy time by saying, "I'll talk about anything you want, what shall we talk about first?" You may have to endure several flare ups, but disarming anger is the first step to rebuilding your line of communication. Anger blocks both listening and thinking. Negotiate for calmness.

5. Protecting yourself from your own anger.
Getting mad immobilizes you. It overloads your system, chases out logical thought, diminishes your self-respect and runs roughshod over the self-respect of others. To avoid fits of anger, anticipate what could go wrong to upset you and think how you'd deal with it. At the first flush of unexpected anger, stop your mind from racing ahead and silently start counting to ten. This gives you a moment to get your thoughts and feelings in order. As you think, so you feel, and as you feel, so you act.

6. Protect yourself against your own anxiety.
When you feel threatened by something you can't control, you experience anxiety, a state that is physically disturbing, emotionally upsetting and mentally disabling. Anxiety is rooted in feelings of insecurity. As your social skills and self-image improve, you feel more secure and are better able to deal with anxiety. Use your strengths to extinguish anxious feelings gradually. For example, if you're fearing having to make a speech, break the task into its elements and start practicing the parts you can do best. Then move to the next safest areas and keep moving until you have overcome all your fears. It's the old military principle of throwing power against weak spots instead of attacking all along the line.

7. Relieving anxiety in others. People who are ridden with anxieties can't do good work. Supervisors should not only refrain from casting a spell of fear over their workers, but should do all they can to ease fears. Being open and honest with them gives them a sense of security, because they know where they stand with you. Calm them down when they're upset, build their self-respect by showing them they can solve their own problems and give them a say in how they do their work -- these are ways supervisors can reduce anxiety among their subordinates.

8. Giving recognition. It sounds contradictory to say that a simple way to assert yourself is to notice sombody else. Yet it's true. When you look people in the eye and give a friendly nod, when you say "Good morning," pause for a handshake or ask "How's the family?" you are not only enhancing their self-respect, but making them aware of you as a leader they respect.

9. Acknowledging what they say. Acknowledging what others say is proof you heard it. Rephrasing it or advancing the thought another step shows you are listening with your head as well as your ears.

Even if you disagree with what is said, acknowledging it shows respect for the other person's right to an opinion and takes the tension out of a potential argument. Be open to the facts, give full weight to another's point of view, and come back with stronger points, if you can.

10. Giving and receiving compliments. Honest praise helps a worker build a positive self-image and maintain self-esteem. You can be sure that your workers accept sincere compliments at full face value, and you should accept compliments with ease and grace. To play them down or reject them out of false modesty demeans both the compliment giver and the compliment receiver.

11. Building your own feelings of self-respect. Living up to what you expect of yourself is what builds your self-respect. Set your standards high enough to be challenging, but realistic enough to be capable of attainment. Your goals should match your potential, and perhaps stretch it a bit.

Self-respect comes from an inner sense of "having your act together," meaning that you are well-organized and moving toward your goals, while respecting the personal goals of others and their right to pursue them.

12. "Ask for the order." That's what sales managers continually impress upon their salesmen. Don't press the application of the principles you have learned in this book so far that they become more important than the ends they are designed to achieve. Create the right kind of environment for your workers, be the right kind of leader, give them the support they need, but in the end, expect them to produce.

20

USING WHAT YOU'VE LEARNED

Reading this book has made you aware of the three basic things you need to do to handle the people side of your job as a supervisor. The exercises gave you an opportunity to see how interacting, confronting and decision sharing apply in relationships with your workers.

Empowering your workers is something like turning the ignition key to start your car. If the car had to run on the starting motor, you wouldn't get very far. But once the engine takes hold, you have a lot of horsepower at your command. You can accelerate, brake and steer to get where you want to go, and the engine does the work. Your people are the engine.

With all the advances in technology, people power is still the driving force of companies and nations. How that power is used is up to supervisors like you, who are in the front lines of management. The kind of work environment you create for the people in your group will shape their attitudes and responses. It all starts with your initiative.

If you tried out the practices suggested as you went through this book, you probably found that they are easier than you at first imagined. The reason is that once workers are empowered and given some say in their jobs, they will begin to manage themselves. The system propels itself.

The hard part is bringing yourself to let it run on its

own. We know how difficult it is for some supervisors to share their authority to make decisions. They have to see substantial rewards ahead for taking the leap.

These rewards are quite real, as we've shown throughout this book. They have been amply proved in a wide range of organizations. The system presented is not some far-out, crackpot idea. Its roots go back to the founding fathers of our country, who proclaimed that all men are created equal. They saw that when people are freed from the shackles of coercive governance, their potential can be released for the common good.

These ideals are applicable to business today. All who are qualified to be hired have the potential to think for themselves. With your guidance, your people can think on the job and contribute to the continuous improvement that organizations are striving to obtain.

Worker empowerment has passed its tests with flying colors. It is poised to become the accepted way to manage people in American industry.

You are coming in at the right time. Start using what you have learned and become one of the new breed of supervisors.   #   #   #

ABOUT THE AUTHORS

LLOYD PRESSEL, Ph.D., is a consultant who has also owned and managed several small businesses, including a machine tool shop and professional services. He was raised on an Iowa farm, was graduated from Drake University and served for four years in the Army. Thereafter, he earned master's and Ph.D. degrees in industrial psychology at Illinois Institute of Technology. He spent his first seven years in business with two leading management engineering firms and then joined Mead Johnson, a pharmaceutical manufacturer, in Evansville, Indiana, as director of organization planning and management development, In 1962, he established his own consulting firm, now headquartered in Bisbee, Arizona. He conducts supervisor training programs and management evaluation studies for a wide variety of organizations throughout the country.

ROBERT H. GARDNER co-founded Gardner, Jones & Company, public relations counsel, and managed it for 30 years until it was acquired by Hill and Knowlton, Inc., where he is now a senior consultant. He advises companies on employee and corporate policies and has developed numerous communications and employee information programs. He is a graduate of Amherst College and a Fellow of the Public Relations Society of America. He has served in the Army.

INDEX

ORDER FORM

Loma Linda Publishers
Box AA
Bisbee, Arizona 85603
Telephone: (612) 432-5361

Please send me the following books:

Number   Total

_____   Supervision for   @ $24.95 each $_____
         Empowered Workers
         By Lloyd Pressel, Ph.D.
         & Robert H. Gardner

_____   The New Creators of   @ $17.95 each $_____
         Empowered Workers
         By Lloyd Pressel, Ph.D.
         & Robert H. Gardner

_____   Supervisor Training   @ $175.00 per $_____
         Seminar Manual (box of 25)
         By Lloyd Pressel, Ph.D.
         (Available only in quantities of 25)

         Shipping and handling charges:(Book Rate) $_____
         $1.75 for first book; $1.50 each additional
         book. $3 per box for manuals.
         $3.00 per book or $5.00 per box for
         priority mail. $_____

TOTAL REMITTANCE
(Check or money order) $_____

   Name: _____

   Address: _____

   City: _____State:_____Zip:_____

Call or write the publisher for VOLUME DISCOUNTS on three or more
copies of any of the above.

ORDER FORM

Loma Linda Publishers
Box AA
Bisbee, Arizona 85603
Telephone: (612) 432-5361

Please send me the following books:

Number   Total

_____   Supervision for   @ $24.95 each $_____
        Empowered Workers
        By Lloyd Pressel, Ph.D.
        & Robert H. Gardner

_____   The New Creators of   @ $17.95 each $_____
        Empowered Workers
        By Lloyd Pressel, Ph.D.
        & Robert H. Gardner

_____   Supervisor Training   @ $175.00 per $_____
        Seminar Manual (box of 25)
        By Lloyd Pressel, Ph.D.
        (Available only in quantities of 25)

        Shipping and handling charges:(Book Rate) $_____
        $1.75 for first book; $1.50 each additional
        book. $3 per box for manuals.
        $3.00 per book or $5.00 per box for
        priority mail. $_____

TOTAL REMITTANCE
(Check or money order) $_____

    Name: _____

    Address: _____

    City: _____State:_____Zip:_____

Call or write the publisher for VOLUME DISCOUNTS on three or more